DATABASE DESIGN FOR INFORMATION RETRIEVAL

DATABASE DESIGN FOR INFORMATION RETRIEVAL

A Conceptual Approach

Raya Fidel

University of Washington
Seattle, Washington

JOHN WILEY & SONS

New York / Chichester / Brisbane / Toronto / Singapore

This publication is designed to provide accurate and
authoritative information in regard to the subject
matter covered. It is sold with the understanding that
the publisher is not engaged in rendering legal, accounting,
or other professional service. If legal advice or other
expert assistance is required, the services of a competent
professional person should be sought. *From a Declaration
of Principles jointly adopted by a Committee of the
American Bar Association and a Committee of Publishers.*

Library of Congress Cataloging in Publication Data:
Fidel, Raya, 1945-
  Database design for information retrieval.

  Includes bibliographies and index.
  1. Data bases.   2. Information storage and retrieval
systems. I. Title. II. Series.
QA76.9.D3F53 1987   005.74   87-12967
ISBN 0-471-82786-X

Printed in the United States of America

10 9 8 7 6 5 4 3 2 1

To my parents
Tova and Eliezer Fidel

PREFACE

Developing a database involves four distinct functions, each building on the previous one: analysis, design, coding, and testing. In the *analysis* stage, the database designer defines what a database should do to make it most useful to potential users by studying user needs, or data requirements analysis, and documentation. During *design*, a process that defines how a database will perform its tasks, the designer concentrates on software and hardware considerations. *Coding* represents the actual implementation of the design. *Testing* is carried out before the full-scale installation of a database to examine how well it will perform.

This book is about the first function—analysis. It explains how to perform data requirements analysis and how to represent the outcome of this analysis in a formal and comprehensive model that is useful for software and hardware considerations. The book is suitable either as a textbook or as a handbook for systems analysts, end users, or information specialists who want to design their own databases.

Books about database design often use highly technical language. An experienced professional may find such shorthand attractive, but jargon often deters the novice. I have, therefore, sought the middle ground by using a nontechnical and jargon-free language that still does not oversimplify concepts and ideas. In that sense this book is elementary: no prior knowledge of systems analysis or computer programming is necessary. However, this is *not* a tutorial on data requirements analysis. No review of existing tools and techniques is provided; instead the book presents a fully developed method for analysis, including "how to" and "why."

The literature on database design most often deals with databases that are built around *processes*, for example, loan transactions or shipment of parts, and that are designed for well-structured organizations. Data requirements analysis for such organizations usually involves creating a model of existing procedures and structures to trace information flow and sequence of routines as they are performed. In a manner of speaking, these analysts are developing databases that *replace* existing information systems.

In contrast, this book covers data requirements analysis and documentation for systems that do not yet exist and for which structure of the information flow is unknown. A good example of this kind of information system is a database for a decision support system, for example, one that provides travel and vacation information, or even one planned to support regulatory functions such as decisions about construction licensing.

Database design first became a focus of interest when computer technology had become advanced enough to facilitate a rapid and efficient processing of a large amount of data. Previously, databases of a sort did exist: a telephone directory, an inventory list, or any payroll system are examples. The development of these kinds of "databases" also required analysis and design, but the amount of data they could store was limited, and their design was performed on an ad hoc basis, following traditional practices.

The first attempts to develop a more systematic approach to the organizing of data for retrieval were catalyzed by computers. Such an approach became necessary as the amount of data that could be handled by a single system grew, and as it became clear that data and procedures had to be expressed in formal representations—the only kind of representation that a computer can "understand."

The design of the first computer databases was the responsibility of programmers. They created data files that were collections of similar kinds of records and, in so doing, performed all four distinct functions required to develop a database. Because of the limited scope of each file, and because of their training, these programmers analyzed data requirements with the software and hardware in mind rather than the needs of the system's users.

Further developments in computer technology paved the way for more sophisticated and complex software. Managers were then forced to realize that the file system is not only limited in its capabilities but also introduces both redundancy and inefficiency. Consequently, the concept of the database as a single, central store of data with multiple uses finally evolved as a realistic and workable goal.

This change in direction has likewise altered the approach of database designers to data requirements analysis. Building a single store of data with multiple uses cannot be done by an ad hoc approach: the amount and diversity of data necessitate a *systematic* method of analysis. Numerous systems have failed to perform to the satisfaction of their users because the analysis of data requirements was not rigorous enough. It became clear that requirements analysis had to be carried out independently of physical design, and that data requirements should affect the selection of software and hardware.

Structured systems analysis emerged in the mid 1970s to answer the need for a systematic methodology. It includes a variety of approaches to data requirement analysis—such as HIPO diagrams, Warnier-Orr diagrams, or action diagrams—each providing tools and techniques for the representation of information flow and procedures in an organization.

Most of the approaches in structured systems analysis represent hierarchical data. These are most suitable for well-structured organizations such as corporations, where the data are likewise structured hierarchically. These approaches become inefficient, however, when nonhierarchical associations exist in the data, a situation typical of databases for decision support systems. One of the approaches that does not require hierarchical relationships is the Entity-Relationship Model, and this approach is used in this book.

Here you will find a step-by-step approach to database design; the chapters are organized to enable a designer or analyst to follow a sequence in the process of data requirements analysis and documentation. You will learn how to collect data about potential information needs, and how to analyze the requirements collected when no apparent structure can be used as a guide. Then suggestions are provided concerning how to develop a data dictionary and a data model—an Entity-Relationship Model—that represents these requirements. Though the text presents the procedures in the sequence in which they will be undertaken, the process of database design is not linear. You are advised, therefore, to complete the book before actually analyzing data requirements for a database; each chapter is clarified by later ones.

This book is a product of cooperative effort. Through their persistent questions, my students at the University of Washington's Graduate School of Library and Information Science helped me to develop the ideas presented here. My colleague Dr. Edmond Mignon provided necessary encouragement. Dr. Irene Travis and Dr. Dagobert Soergel thoroughly reviewed early drafts of the book; their incisive criticism and suggestions, as well as warm collegial support, were a motive force for this work. Tamara Turner rendered invaluable assistance in the preparation of the manuscript for publication.

RAYA FIDEL

Seattle, Washington
October 1987

CONTENTS

DATABASE DESIGN FOR INFORMATION RETRIEVAL

1

INTRODUCTION

The conceptual approach to database design provides a systematic method for choosing what should be represented in a database and in what manner. This chapter explains why it is important to use a systematic approach and introduces two basic characteristics of a database: enterprise and environments. Then the three levels of design—internal, external, and conceptual—are defined. Taken cumulatively, the conceptual decisions create a schema. This book is about the development of this conceptual schema, which begins with the study of the problem, then proceeds to represent data in formal terms, and concludes with the selection of rules for data collection.

THE SIGNIFICANCE OF A CONCEPTUAL APPROACH

At the earliest stage of database design, all that is known is the purpose that a database is supposed to fulfill. The details of its contents and the specifics of its use are not yet well defined. In this book, this stage of the process is examined in the context of decision support systems, or databases that support decision making of a fairly well defined nature. An example would be a "talent bank" that is operated by a corporation to support decisions about personnel placement, or a database that provides information to convention planners.

Most methodologies for database design assume that the system is being built to support an administrative process, and that the design process can proceed from administrative requirements and the analysis of information flow within an organization. These techniques of "structural analysis" are well documented in the database literature, and we will survey them only briefly in Chapter 2 while discussing how to gather data from the environment. In contrast, this book provides a guide to database designers for carrying out requirements analysis and database specifications for *decisions* (rather than processes) in nonstructural information environments.

This is not a "how-to" book, but a database designer can gather a general understanding of how to carry out the initial stage of database design. We do provide a method for determining what information should be stored in a database and how this information can be best represented.

These processes of requirements analysis and database specifications in nonstructural information environments have been largely ignored by the database literature. Still, much experience in these processes has been gathered during the construction of *bibliographic* databases: Information specialists have been constructing databases that represent the world of print for the last four decades. Here is a good example of a nonstructural information environment, and the vast experience that has been accumulated is extremely valuable. Unfortunately, the practices and procedures emerging from this experience over the years have been applied only to bibliographic databases.

In this book I have taken the experience gathered in the construction of bibliographic databases and used it to develop a general method that is applicable to databases of *any* kind. I use the approach to database design developed by Cerri and colleagues [1] as an overall framework. This combination of long experience in database design and a new theoretical analysis provides the conceptual approach of this book—an approach crucial to the early stage of database design. A hypothetical example will best explain what is involved.

Suppose the administrators of a visitors' center in a medium-sized city are asked to construct a database that provides information about "what is going on" in the city. (*Note:* The terms *data* and *information* are used interchangeably in this book.) Suppose also that, for this purpose, the center gets access to a computer and is given a budget both to acquire software and to arrange for training from software vendors. A person from the staff is assigned to design the database.

The first question that the designer should ask is, What is the "universe" to be represented in the database? In other words, what sorts of events, activities, and other attractions of the city should be considered, what details of these matters are meaningful, and what is the best way to present the details from the point of view of a visitor's needs? More specifically, the designer must decide whether restaurants, concert halls, and so on, are of interest, and if so, what visitors need to know about them exactly; how items of data from different sources (e.g., restaurants, transportation) relate to one another; and how best to organize the database so that information is easily retrieved.

How can the designer take a *systematic* approach to answer these questions? A systematic approach provides an orderly and comprehensive check and refinement on personal intuition. The framework established in this way saves a good deal of trial-and-error guesswork when the decisions that have been made must be stated in formal terms, as required for storage in a database.

Why is a systematic approach required to define the "universe" of such a database?

It is always more efficient to follow some kind of procedure when large amounts of data are to be collected and stored. Creating a database for information retrieval means representing real-life objects in rigorously structured and formal terms. These objects are not under our control and are frequently unpredictable and idiosyncratic. We need a procedure to capture these "unruly" objects so that information about them can be stored in our neatly structured and orderly database.

As an example of objects' unpredictability, suppose the designer in the visitors' center decides to first collect data about restaurants. From his travel experience he concludes that visitors most often need to know the type of food that is served in each restaurant (e.g., Chinese, bar-b-que) and the average price of a dinner. To collect data for the restaurant portion of the database, he devises a form with three columns: restaurant's name, type of food, and price. Data collected from each restaurant are entered in one row.

After 10 hours of recording information about restaurants, the designer comes across a promotional leaflet from the Willow Tree Restaurant: It serves Chinese food and the average price of a dinner is $10, but on Friday it serves only bar-b-que and the average price is $7. How can he represent this information?

The designer may have various suggestions. He can assume, for instance, that the Willow Tree is actually two restaurants: the first one, and a "new" restaurant that is open only on Friday. He can then enter information about this new restaurant (Willow Tree, bar-b-que, $7) in the next row. This "solution" results immediately in two problems: (1) there are now two restaurants with the same name, and (2) visitors must be advised that the first restaurant is closed on Friday and that the second one is open only on Friday.

To solve the first problem the designer may decide to create the following rule: Two or more restaurants have the same name if they are located in the same place; but they may or may not serve the same type of food, and they may charge different prices. This rule may get in the way later on when he records information about restaurants that have the same name but are located in different places (e.g., chain restaurants)—in which case a new rule must be created and all data recorded up to that point must be brought into compliance with it.

To solve the second problem, the designer may decide to record the day of the week on which a restaurant is open in an additional column on the data recording form. At this point he has to go back and record days for all the previous restaurants, an extremely demanding task if the Willow Tree Restaurant is 500th on the list and most data were received over the telephone.

No matter how the designer solves the Willow Tree irregularity, the rule he chooses must not contradict any rules already established and it must be easily applied to all later restaurants as well. With each additional restaurant, additional irregularities may be discovered that will result in yet more rules. If the database is of any size and scope, sooner or later the network of rules will become too complex to handle.

The designer in this example will be much better off if he develops rules and conventions for representing restaurants in a systematic manner, so that rules and conventions can be easily checked for consistency before data are actually collected. For example, the designer would save a lot of work if, while designing the data collection form, he followed this procedure: "For each data collection table, check whether each distinct element in the first column has only one element corresponding to it in each of the other columns." Such a procedure would have led him to check before he collected data whether restaurants always serve the same type of food and whether they always charge the same price. He could then use his experience and intuition, or information available to him, to define common irregularities in restaurants and to develop a unified set of rules for recording data.

The conceptual approach presented in this book facilitates the development of such rules. But before we introduce the approach, we need to clarify some basic concepts and to define more rigorously which aspects of database design are covered by this approach.

DATABASES, THEIR ENTERPRISE
AND ENVIRONMENTS

Although we have already used the term *database,* it is not too late to define it. For our discussion we can use a very broad definition: *A database is a store of data about a selected part of the real world that is intended to be used for particular purposes.* Thus, an electronic telephone directory, a state archive, or the reference books in a library are all databases.

From this definition it is clear that a database differs from other data stores in two ways:

1. The data stored have to be about a part of the real world. This subset is called the *enterprise* that is represented in the database.

2. The data are stored to answer information needs arising for particular purposes. Each such purpose defines a particular *environment* of the database.

Among the first specifications that a database designer needs to clarify are the enterprise and the environments of a database. These should be defined in the most explicit and specific terms possible. Note also that the terms *enterprise* and *environments* have here a somewhat broader interpretation than in their common use.

The database for the visitors' center has a city as its enterprise. Let us say, for instance, that the center is in Seattle. Having a Seattle database implies that the data stored in it are all related, in one way or another, to the city of Seattle. Such a definition of an enterprise is too broad, but the designer needs to examine the multiple environments of the database before he tries to limit the enterprise any further.

It is extremely important to define environments as explicitly as possible because many of the decisions in later stages of the design will be based on the characteristics of the particular environments involved. Typically, the enterprise and environments are given to the designer by the body that decided to build the database. Sometimes, however, determining the environments of a database becomes an involved process of definition and redefinition. Databases that provide general information to the public are the most problematical because the reality with which these databases interact is so complicated.

For instance, when the designer examines the purpose of the Seattle database (to provide information about what is going on in the city), he might immediately conclude that it has one environment: tourists. Then he ponders the needs of Seattle residents, who are always looking for ways to entertain themselves as well as guests from out of town. Now he is up to two environments. But residents may want information about the city that is not relevant for tourists (e.g., data about social and housing services). By adding some data, therefore, the designer can provide residents with answers to their information needs about the city.

This expansion in the number of environments is in line with current views of data storage and retrieval. In fact, many experts see the concept *database* as representing a modern approach to information systems that, unlike the traditional one, encourages the use of a pool of data for a *variety* of purposes. One may say that the designer has chosen to construct a *shared* database, which is a database with more than one environment. This shared database is also an *integrated* database because it puts two seemingly different data stores—one for tourists, the other for residents— into one data store and thus eliminates redundancy.

Suppose the city library, rather than the visitors' center, is asked to design the Seattle database. This library is located in the city hall and the chosen designer realizes that people in the city administration could readily use a database providing information about institutions and events in the city. Thus he decides to add a third environment: city administrators.

At this point the designer has defined three environments for the Seattle database. Now he needs to check whether these are indeed distinct environments.

First, he examines the tourist and resident environments. Analyzing the kinds of questions that visitors and residents are likely to bring to the database, he concludes that the two environments are very similar. After all, most people need the same information about concerts or movies, whether they are tourists or residents. Tourists are probably not interested in the availability of social services and residents may find information about a tour in their own neighborhood irrelevant, but the nature of the information needed is almost the same: both tourists and residents use services offered by the city and its institutions. The designer, therefore, decides to consolidate these two environments into one that he labels *the clientele environment*. It includes all groups of people looking for information about the services available in the city (in the broadest sense of the concept).

The designer then maintains that city administrators are part of the organization. They are interested in the provision of services, rather than in using them, at least in their capacity as city administrators. They are in effect part of the city and information about their activities might even be included in the database. He concludes that the administrators should be approached as a distinct environment, which he labels *the administration environment*.

The distinction between the environments is important and far-reaching. At this point it is sufficient to emphasize that even though the same data may be stored for both environments, the information will be looked at in completely different ways. For example, suppose restaurants need a license to serve alcoholic beverages. Tourists may ask the database for the address and telephone number of, say, a French restaurant that is licensed. As far as they are concerned, they only need to know whether or not a restaurant is licensed. Administrators, on the other hand, may want to know how many licenses had been issued in the last month, or when the license of a particular restaurant needs to be renewed. Their information needs about licensing are different from a tourist's, yet the database could be designed to answer both types of requests.

You may have noticed that even though environments are defined in terms of "people," they are not defined by individuals but rather by the roles or tasks individuals perform. Environments are defined by information needs generated by these roles or tasks. A city administrator may belong to the administration environment when he checks the licensing status of a restaurant, but to the clientele environment a moment later when he plans his next business lunch and wants to find a nice French restaurant that serves wine. It is important to remember, then, that while environments are labeled after groups of people, one person, and in fact, a whole group of people, may belong to more than one environment.

Now that the database's environments are defined, the designer again may examine the enterprise of the database. One way to redefine the enterprise is to state that the database stores all data about the city of Seattle and of interest to its administrators or to people who use the city's services. Alternately, the designer may choose to be more explicit, and list the types of services to be presented in the database.

While it is important to define the environments of a database rigorously, the definition of its enterprise may be modified once the database is actually designed. In this example, therefore, we will now assume that the designer feels ready to design the database. But first he needs to know what is involved in this process.

LEVELS OF DESIGN

To understand the responsibilities of the designer of a database, especially in relation to functions performed by other people such as software vendors or data processing personnel at the city's computer center, it is useful to distinguish among the three levels of design, the internal, external, and conceptual. As we shall see later, it is important to separate the decisions made on each level from those made on the others.

Internal Level

The internal level involves decisions concerning *how the data are actually stored*. Database designers can turn to the internal design only after they have decided on the enterprise that should be represented in the database and how to represent each element in the enterprise.

To illustrate the nature of decisions made on this level, imagine that the city database is designed to be a manual (not computerized) database. Some examples of decisions the designer makes with regard to the method of data storage are:

1. The information about each restaurant is recorded on a 3 × 5 card with a hole at the lower center and the cards are kept in wooden drawers with a rod holding them. Such a decision affects the physical aspects of data storage and may, therefore, be considered as a "physical level" decision (a level we will not discuss further).

2. Each card for a restaurant has a certain format: the name of the restaurant at the top, telephone number below on the right-hand side of the card, address on the left-hand side, and so on.

3. Since access will be possible by type of food and by price (a decision made earlier), each restaurant has two additional cards: one with its type of food printed on top and another with the price.

4. The type of food and the price cards for each restaurant have

only the name of the relevant restaurants as additional information.

5. The type of food and the price entries are typed in red ribbon.
6. All the cards with information about restaurants, and only these cards, are interfiled in one set of drawers.

These examples show that decisions on the internal level relate to issues such as: (1) the medium on which data are stored, (2) the format in which data are stored, and methods used to provide access to data, (3) indexes, (4) amount of information provided with each entry, (5) form of entries, and (6) internal organization of entries.

External Level

The external level involves decisions concerning the *particular views of the data that are geared to specific purposes.* Decisions on this level guide a database designer in the provision of information; they determine how to retrieve and display information in a manner that is useful for each group of users having a particular view of the data. Such decisions can be made only after the enterprise of a database has been decided on.

Imagine this time that the city database is to be computerized. The data are stored in the computer in a manner the data processing staff felt was most efficient. The following are examples of decisions the designer made on the external level:

1. To request information about a restaurant, a requester must know the name of the restaurant, or the type of food it serves, or the price it charges. In other words, the database accommodates for a view according to which at least one of these elements is known.
2. While a menu-driven interaction is suggested, users who are experienced with the database can interact directly with a preset group of commands.
3. The database is "partitioned" into three segments, or files: the first arranged by the restaurant's name, the second by

type of food, and the last by price. A user should first "open" the relevant file and only then retrieve information. (The term *users* in this book usually means *end users*, in other words, people whose information needs are supposed to be answered by the database.)

4. A user can find restaurants that serve two (or more) particular types of food, or all the restaurants that serve at least one of two (or more) types of food; but a user cannot look for restaurants serving a particular type of food that charge a designated price.

5. The display of information retrieved varies according to the following views: an alphabetical list of restaurants' names, a list of restaurants' names arranged by their address, and so on.

These examples show that decisions on the external level concern issues such as: (1) a means to express a request, (2) a means to ask questions in a language that the computer "understands," or an interface language, (3) a picture of the arrangement of the data, (4) a picture of the possible manipulation of data, and (5) formats for display of answers.

Conceptual Level

The conceptual level involves decisions concerning *the representation of the entire enterprise in the database*. In other words, the designer looks at the data from a perspective that is independent of the way they are stored and of the ways they are viewed by various users. Conceptual decisions are thus independent of internal and external level decisions.

Consider again the city database, whether computerized or manual. Decisions on the conceptual level include:

1. What elements of information about restaurants should be stored (e.g., name, type of food, name of owner, capacity)?

2. How should the name of a restaurant be determined, or "established" (e.g., use the name that appears in the telephone

book, ask the owner, or use the name written on a restaurant's sign)?

3. How should types of food be recorded (e.g., use the type given by restaurant owners, or check against a pre-established list)?

4. How should a list of food types be built?

5. How many types of food can a restaurant have?

These examples should make it clear that decisions on the conceptual level are independent of those on other levels. For instance, the decision about the rules to establish the name of a restaurant are not affected by the medium on which the data are stored, nor by how information is displayed to users.

While the conceptual level is independent of the internal and external levels, at the same time it is also the only link between those two levels; it serves as a "stable" insulation between them. The representation of the entire enterprise is much more stable, or much less likely to be changed, than decisions made at the internal and external levels, which are somewhat dynamic. For example, the decision (on the conceptual level) that a restaurant's type of food should be included in the database and that it should fit into a pre-established list of food types is not likely to be changed during the lifetime of the database. In contrast, the designer may eventually decide (on the internal level) to type this entry with a green ribbon. Or, he may decide to make it possible to find restaurants serving a particular type of food that charge a designated price (a decision on the external level).

The bridge provided by the conceptual level between the external and internal levels, does not imply, however, that a change in one of those levels forces a change in the other. For instance, the designer's decision to present the type of food in green letters has no effect on user ability to retrieve information about the type of food because food type is defined on the conceptual level regardless of the color of the letters in which it is typed on the cards. Similarly, adding a view that makes it possible to get a list of types of food and the charges that are involved does not have any impact on the color in which entries are typed or on similar decisions on the internal level.

A person who is primarily responsible for decisions on the conceptual level is called an *enterprise administrator* (or a *data administrator*). This person is also responsible for the database's integrity and security. To secure the *integrity* of a database, an enterprise administrator must keep the conceptual plan current, consistent, and correct. Database *security* is achieved by protecting the database from unauthorized users.

MANUAL AND COMPUTERIZED DATABASES

It is common to separate design considerations for automated systems from those of manual ones. Dealing with database design on the conceptual level, though, lets us promote the notion that the nature of many design considerations and decisions is common to manual and computerized databases. The conceptual approach is virtually identical for both types of databases because it is independent of the external and the internal approaches. By examining the preceding examples one can see that principles used on the internal and external levels can also apply to both manual and computerized systems. For a variety of reasons, however, this book will assume the databases under discussion are computerized.

First, automated systems are more powerful than manual systems: They store more data and support manipulation of data more easily than manual systems do. In addition to special capabilities provided by computerized systems, such as searching capabilities that are highly flexible, computers perform clerical processes much faster than humans and, thus, can easily execute tasks that would require a prohibitive amount of time in manual systems.

Second, most databases of reasonable size, if not all of them, are actually designed to be operated on a computer. With the wide use of microcomputers, and the large variety of software available for them, even a small organization or one with limited financial resources is likely to select an automated option for its database.

Third, from a methodical point of view, it is better to build

good habits by having a computerized database in mind because
its design forces explicit definition of every element in the design.
Manual systems seem immediate and concrete and, therefore, in-
duce the illusion that they can be designed using intuition only.
It seems easy to introduce changes because all the information
and processes are readily and concretely available. Also, interaction with manual systems usually means that users process some
information on their own and therefore a rigorous design is not
required.

In contrast, building a computerized database requires clear
thinking about options and possible uses because the information
and the processes involved are abstract and need to be expressed
in formal terms. We also expect computerized databases to provide the most specific and accurate answer to a user request without any requirement for further processing of information. Thus
we deal in this book with computerized systems primarily because their design makes us proceed in a systematic manner and
use a formal approach—a procedure that is recommended for the
design of *any* type of database.

THE CONCEPTUAL SCHEMA

Issues on the conceptual level can be separated into three con-
secutive processes: (1) study of the problem, (2) representation of
data in formal terms, and (3) selection of rules for data collection.

The first process, the *study of the problem,* involves explorations
to find out what kind of information is needed—the requirements
that users bring to the database. This process is often called *requirements collection, requirements analysis,* or *data requirements analysis.* In this process database designers collect user requirements
and analyze them to identify the individual problems a database
is supposed to solve.

This task involves three steps. First, the designers identify typical representatives from the user population and ask them about
their potential requirements. They record information needs expressed by these users as fully as possible on requirements collection forms. Second, the designers organize these data in a useful
manner: Sentences in users' statements are recorded and organized to eliminate redundancy in expressed needs and to provide

some structure and consistency in the information about user needs they contain. Finally, from these sentences they construct a data dictionary that includes definitions for each element of data identified, such as the location or the quality of a restaurant, and an operations dictionary that describes and defines the operations, or activities, associated with the enterprise of the database, and the data associated with each operation.

The first step is described in Chapter 2, the second in Chapter 3, and the last step is discussed in Chapter 4.

In the second process, *representing the data in formal terms*, designers begin to build a model to represent the enterprise: They use the information needs that were identified in the previous process to formulate the elements that should be included in the database and how they should relate to one another. This process is discussed in Chapters 5 and 6. The outcome is a graphic representation of the elements and their relationships shown by an Entity-Relationship Diagram.

The third process is the *selection of rules*. Here designers define rules for the representation of the elements formulated before, and for the ways they can be related to one another. This process is delineated in Chapter 7. The formal representation of elements and their relationships, and the rules devised, together create *the conceptual schema:* a diagramatic presentation, or a formal outline, that explicitly expresses all the decisions on the conceptual level. The conceptual schema is sometimes called *the data model* or *the logical model* of a database.

While each process in this design routine is based on the previous one, in practice deviation from the strict order may be necessary. A later process may be initiated before the previous one is completed, and earlier processes can sometimes be completed only after the later ones have progressed. In fact, the whole routine of building the conceptual schema most often requires checking, rechecking, and modification of decisions made in previous processes. The transition from one process to another is largely based on intuition, and each increment in such a transition should be validated and rechecked. To aid such validations, Chapter 8 lists and discusses features that are essential to the evaluation of the conceptual schema.

Validation of decisions and a repeated check of them for consistency are extremely important to the success of the conceptual schema. First, the conceptual schema needs to be consistent within itself. In other words, rules devised in the third process (selection of rules) should not contradict any of the elements—or the relationships among them—that were defined in the preceding processes. Second, the schema should reflect user requirements as closely as possible. Thus, even when designers devise rules, they may need to check particular requirements and their sources.

One of the pitfalls of this method is the subjectivity involved in the decision about how far to proceed with rechecking and modifications, or when to cut corners. By searching for perfection, a designer could easily turn a medium-sized database into a lifetime project. While there are no straightforward guidelines about how far to go, there is one useful principle: No database design can be perfect; some designs are better than others, but there is no "best" design for any given database.

This principle is alarming and comforting at the same time. It tells us, on the one hand, that any given database can be improved. No matter how much thought and effort went into the design of a database, there is always more to do to make it better. On the other hand, we can be assured that we can never design an "ideal" database—so we might as well design a "good" one and know that we have accomplished a worthwhile goal.

Ultimately, outcomes of almost any decision we make on the conceptual level will have advantages and disadvantages. To secure a successful design, we must be able to see clearly the full impact of every decision, and weigh it against our priorities for the design of a given database. In other words, to build a "good" database, a designer must understand the tradeoffs involved in each decision and be able to judge them in light of the goals set for the database.

SUMMARY

The conceptual approach helps database designers to develop a systematic procedure to support decision making at the earliest stage of the database design process. This approach guides designers in deciding what data are available, how to collect them, and how to organize them for efficient and useful retrieval. While a systematic approach is essential to any design process, the often unpredictable and idiosyncratic nature of the data that are collected makes it the only workable approach for the design of most databases.

A *database* is a store of data about a selected part of the real world that is intended to be used for particular purposes. This part of the real world is called the *enterprise* of the database. Each particular purpose for which data are stored defines a particular *environment* of the database. The enterprise and the environments should be defined in the most explicit and specific terms possible and at the very first stage of the database design.

Most modern databases are *shared* and *integrated* because they have more than one environment, and because they put together seemingly different data stores into one data store, eliminating redundancy.

Database design comprises three levels of design:

1. *The internal level* concerns how the data are actually stored. For example, the format in which data are stored, or the type of indexes.

2. *The external level* concerns the particular views of the data that are geared to specific purposes. For example, a means to express a request, or formats for display of answers.

3. *The conceptual level* concerns the representation of the entire enterprise in the database. For example, rules to establish names, or rules about the use of terms.

The conceptual level is independent of the internal and external levels but at the same time is the only link between the two. This book focuses on the conceptual level of database design. Even though design decisions on this level are common to both manual and computerized systems, here we use only automated systems as examples.

REFERENCE

1. Cerri, S., Ed. 1983. *Methodology and tools for data base design.* New York: North-Holland.

2

METHODS OF COLLECTING USER REQUIREMENTS

The first step in requirements analysis is to identify a representative sample of users and to collect information about data requirements from them. For the sample to be representative it should be drawn with the composition of the environment in mind as it relates to the functions the database is supposed to support: Each type of user is defined by and linked with the functions he is supposed to perform.

If an environment is structured, such as at banks or universities, a functional chart is created. This chart guides the identification of distinct user types—types that guide the breakdown of each function to its operations. Unstructured environments, such as those involving customers or students, require the creation of a tentative structure that is guided by intuition and commonsense. Functions, types of users, and their associations are further refined as requirements analysis progresses. Requirements are most often collected through interviews that are open ended, yet specific in nature.

The first process on the conceptual level, the study of the problem, is composed of a series of data analyses to find out what kind of information is needed. In other words, database designers explore the needs of potential users—those who participate in the environments of a database—to discover their requirements for the database. In a more refined manner, we can say that designers find out what "picture" of the enterprise (which belongs to the real world) they want to construct in a database so that users who are part of a database environment can retrieve useful information.

Consider our example of the Seattle database. The data that eventually will be stored in the database concern the city, its activities, and services. We have also defined two environments: the clientele and the administration. Now we are ready to uncover the information needs of potential users.

Our plan is to identify a sample of potential users, question them about their information needs, and then organize their answers in a manner that is useful to the design of a database. The first decision to be made is, should we explore requirements of users in both environments at the same time or should we study each environment separately?

Intuitively, it makes sense to approach each environment separately because requirements proposed by tourists or residents are different from those administrators would propose. We could have come to the same conclusion if we had remembered that an environment is determined by the nature of the information needs arising from a particular purpose. We set the boundaries of environments according to the information requirements of their users. In other words, by definition, users in one environment have information needs that are different from those of users in another environment. Therefore, designers should study one environment at a time.

SELECTION OF A USER SAMPLE

The next question is how to identify a sample of potential users. There is no rigorous method that can always guarantee designers that the sample they derive is a "good" one, but we can sketch a few general guidelines.

The size of the sample is most often determined by the resources available for requirements analysis. Unlike for tests and surveys, users in a sample *should not* be selected randomly. This notion may seem unacceptable to trained interviewers, but they must recall that database designers are not establishing evidence of some sort but rather exploring information needs of a particular group of users. The most important task is, therefore, to select representatives from all the subgroups of users within each environment.

To sample users, then, a designer must identify subgroups of users from which to select representatives. Such an identification, however, means going back to basic definitions. We recall here that an environment is defined by some purpose for which information is needed. In fact, we can determine whether or not a person is a user (in other words, whether or not he belongs to an environment) by checking whether or not he is involved in performing a function that relates to the purpose that defines an environment. It makes sense, therefore, to define subgroups according to the functions that are carried out to fulfill a purpose that defines an environment. Going to museums, or riding a cable car, are examples of functions performed to fulfill the purpose of touring a city—a purpose that defines the clientele environment in our example.

A useful procedure to identify user subgroups within an environment is to list all the functions that are involved in accomplishing a purpose. Subgroups of users can then be identified by finding out what types of users are performing each function. A designer can then create a cross-tabulation of user and function, and mark the functions performed by each type of user, as shown in Figure 2.1.

The cross-tabulation guarantees that users who are selected from each subgroup indeed represent a large range of functions. If we had, for example, tourists, residents, reviewers, owners, and so on, included in a list of subgroups, we would be likely to forget to include a restaurant owner when addressing the function "reviewing a restaurant." Some restaurant owners, however, are accustomed to reviewing new restaurants in town, and their information needs are probably different from those of regular restaurant reviewers. The cross-tabulation ensures that the in-

Environment: Clientele				
User ⟍ Function	Tourists	Residents	Reviewers	Owners
Going to a restaurant	X	X	X	X
Dining in a restaurant	X	X	X	X
Reviewing a restaurant			X	X
Running a restaurant				X
...				

Figure 2.1. User/function cross-tabulation

formation needs of an owner about how to review a restaurant are addressed. Moreover, it indicates that the sample should include at least one restaurant owner who is interested in reviewing restaurants.

As we see next, our strategy for creating user/function cross-tabulation strongly depends on the character of the environment. Those environments that have some structure, such as the city administration, can lead us in selecting the functions and types of user. When we select functions and users from an environment that seems disorganized, such as tourists or residents, we have to rely on our intuition and commonsense.

Sampling Structured Environments

When designers select a sample of users from a structured environment, they use the structure of the environment to guide a systematic compilation of a comprehensive list of functions and users. They first define the subject areas that the database is designed to cover. Then they prepare a functional chart of the environment and follow that structure to identify functions and users. Functions can be further decomposed, or broken down, to individual operations that are relevant to each subject area.

Subject Areas in the Enterprise. On a conceptual level, a designer must deal with each individual subject area separately. The advantages of such an approach for clarifying concepts should be clear from the database example we have been using. Although that database is a city database that stores information about everything that is going on in Seattle, we have used only the restaurant subject area in our discussions.

Partitioning the databases subject into specific subject areas is also helpful during the design process. It is overwhelming, if not impossible, to analyze simultaneously the data requirements created by one user group's desire to know about a variety of subject areas (e.g., restaurants, movies, concerts, transportation, or social services). Instead, a designer should investigate each such subject area separately, and within each environment.

In other words, when we develop a database that stores data for a variety of users and a variety of purposes, we build each portion of it separately. For each environment–subject area combination we build a separate part of the conceptual schema. Thus we create the (1) administration–restaurants schema, (2) administration–social services schema, (3) clientele–restaurants schema, (4) clientele–social services schema, and so on. Only at that point do we integrate the local schemata into a global schema, as explained in Chapter 6.

Once designers have selected the subject areas within a database, or those suitable for independent analysis, they can proceed to the next step: uncovering the structure of the environment in a manner that is useful for requirements collection.

Functions Analysis of an Environment. To keep terminology simple we can refer to structured environments as *organizations*. In our example, the administration environment is an organization, and requirements collection for this environment should be guided by its structure.

Most organizations have organizational charts that reflect their administrative structures. Such a chart designates the various departments and their hierarchical relationships with each other. Figure 2.2 is an example of an organizational chart for a hypothetical city. For two reasons, however, this chart, is not appropriate for requirements analysis.

First, the detail is insufficient to identify types of users. We can assume, for example, that administrators in the Licenses and Consumer Affairs department are interested in using our database. But we cannot assume that this department represents only

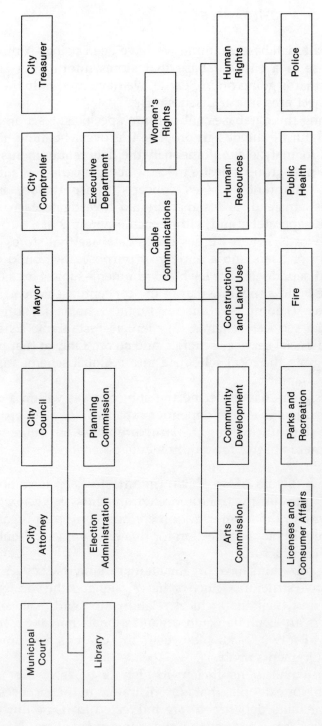

Figure 2.2. The organizational chart of a hypothetical city

24

one type of user. Various administrators in this department probably have different information needs because they represent more than one type of user. Ideally, therefore, we would like to have an organizational chart detailed enough to include individual job titles such as fire marshal, human relations representative, housing/zoning inspector, or environmental specialist.

While organizational charts are usually drawn in a treelike structure, the level of detail such charts can convey is limited. Another technique for representing an organizational structure—and, in fact, any hierarchical structure—is to list the items in a linear fashion with indentations that symbolize hierarchical relationships. Incidentally, librarians are more familiar with this technique of representing hierarchical relationships because it is used in most classification schemes. Figure 2.3 shows the organizational chart of the same hypothetical city, with the entries for some departments presented in more detail. More than one person may hold each job title.

The second reason the organizational chart shown in Figure 2.3 fails is that it does not give information about the *functions* that are performed in the city administration. For that we need a *functional chart*, which presents the functions that are performed in an organization and their relationships to one another. Some organizations may have already prepared the functional chart for their organization, but often a member of the team that designs a database is asked to develop one.

There are various methods for analyzing the functional structure of an organization, and this task usually requires the expert knowledge of a systems analyst. The kind of analysis that is required is often called *structured analysis, structured system analysis,* or *structured design.*

It is beyond the scope of this book to explain or describe functions analysis. A number of books on this subject have been published—such as the introductory text by Martin and McClure [1]—and the interested reader may want to consult them. To illustrate the nature of functional charts, however, Figure 2.4 provides an example of portions of a functional chart for our hypothetical city.

In this figure, the major functions are identified: functions that relate to issuing standards and regulations, or Regulatory Func-

Municipal Court
City Attorney
City Council
   Election Administration
   Library
   Planning Commission
   Executive Department
      Cable Communications
      Women's Rights
Mayor
   Arts Commission
   Community Development
   Construction and Land Use
      Permits and Plans
      Inspections
         Construction Inspections
            Building Inspector
      Plans Examination
   Fire
   Human Resources
   Human Rights
   Licenses and Consumer Affairs
      Licenses
         Licenses and Standards Inspector
         Licenses Officer
      Consumer Affairs
         Counselor
   Parks and Recreation
   Police
   Public Health
City Comptroller
City Treasurer

Figure 2.3. The organizational chart of a hypothetical city, presented linearly

tions; functions that are involved in processes to enforce standards and regulations, or Enforcement Functions; and functions that are carried out to help the general public, or Aid Functions. Major functions are frequently derived from the goals or mission of an organization.

Functions within each of these categories are recorded on the second level. Regulatory Functions, for example, include only one secondary function (Develop standards and codes), while Enforcement Functions include two. Functions listed on the third

Regulatory Functions
Develop standards and codes
    Provide safety standards
    Provide taxation standards

Enforcement Functions
Inspection
    Safety inspection
    Tax Inspection
    Security inspection
    Housing and zoning inspection
    Environmental standards inspection
    Building codes inspection
    Public health inspection
    Discrimination inspection
Issue licenses

Aid Functions
Provide services
    Provide legal services
    Provide housing services
    Provide information services
    Provide health services
    Provide social services
    Provide recreational services
Provide protection
    Physical damage
    Discrimination

Figure 2.4. The functional chart of a hypothetical city

level represent the next step of breaking down functions into their components. This breakdown can continue to whatever level the designer of the database chooses. Indeed, as we discuss later, an organization's functional structure can be analyzed all the way down to individual operations, or activities.

The example presented in Figure 2.4 is an oversimplified version of a functional chart. Such charts often represent relationships among functions as well as listing the functions themselves. For example, the order in which various functions take place can be shown to make clear that no inspection can take place before standards and codes have been developed. To do this the chart must specify that Enforcement and Aid Functions cannot be carried out before relevant Regulatory Functions are performed. Alternatively a relationship can be established by representing information flow among functions. One could, say, show that data collected in the inspection functions are used to issue licenses.

In Figure 2.4, however, we chose not to represent relationships among functions. Databases that are designed to provide information about a variety of functions and relationships require complex functional analyses and charts. These in turn require a display that is much more sophisticated than the hierarchy shown here. Possible tools include data-flow diagrams, Warnier-Orr diagrams, or action diagrams.

Before we develop a detailed functional structure, we should stop on an intermediate level and check which functions are relevant to the database that is being designed. If we construct a functional chart solely for the purpose of database design, we do not want it expanded to include functions that obviously are not relevant to the database.

For example, the functions on the first level (see Figure 2.4) are all relevant to the restaurant subject area of our database. Regulatory Functions, as well as Enforcement and Aid Functions, are part of dealing with restaurants. On the second level, however, we find functions that are not pertinent to our "what is going on in Seattle" database (e.g., Provide safety standards, Provide taxation standards). It is advisable to stop at this point and eliminate functions that are not part of the enterprise, *as we view it from the standpoint of a database.*

It should be noted that, in practice, functions analysis of an organization is performed simultaneously for *all* the subject areas to be covered by a database. While it is important to keep the subject areas separated on the conceptual level, the analysis is time-consuming and requires constant interaction with administrators. A designer would not want, therefore, to construct a new functional chart for every new subject in a database. For purposes of illustration only, we assume here that our database is concerned only with information about restaurants.

Definition of Sections and Functions. Once the functional chart is completed, it is time to make the connection between functions and the sections in the organization that perform them.

This is a natural step because the functions analysis was performed to find out the types of users, and the functions they perform that are relevant to the database.

First, the designer constructs a section/function cross-tabulation that indicates which functions are performed by each section of the organization. This cross-tabulation guides, in turn, the construction of a user/operation cross-tabulation. For this purpose the functional chart needs to be "annotated," indicating which departments and programs are responsible for the performance of each function. In addition, the job titles of the persons who perform the function under which a department is listed are indicated for each program.

An example of such annotation is presented in Figure 2.5. City departments are listed under each function, and for some, the names of programs within a department are added in parentheses. To illustrate the degree of detail that might be needed in such annotations, the job titles of persons who perform a function are enumerated for the Inspection function. These are placed after the name of the program.

Examining this annotated chart we can immediately see that (1) some functions are carried out by more than one department, and (2) some departments perform more than one function. For example, three departments provide protection against discrimination: the Municipal Court, the Human Rights, and the Women's Rights departments. On the other hand, the Licenses and Consumer Affairs Department inspects taxes, issues licenses, and provides information.

In practice, such an annotated chart is too long and complex to be useful as a display. We want, therefore, to annotate the functional chart to a certain level of detail, say, to the department level, and then record programs directly on a section/function cross-tabulation.

Figure 2.6 is an example of such cross-tabulation for the restaurant section of our city database. Each function in the functional chart is matched against departments and programs in the organization. To keep this illustration manageable, only the Construction and Land Use Department is presented by its programs while other departments are recorded as a whole.

The importance of such cross-tabulation should be clear. Only

Inspection

Safety
  Fire (Engineering and Compliance/Fire Marshal)
Taxes
  Licenses and Consumer Affairs (Licenses/Licenses and Standards Inspector)
Security
  Police (Inspectional services/Police Officer)
Housing and Zoning
  Construction and Land Use (Inspections/Housing and Zoning Inspector)
Environmental Standards
  Construction and Land Use (Plans Examination/Environmental Specialist)
Building Codes
  Construction and Land Use (Construction Inspection/Building Inspector)
Public Health
  Health (City Services/Environmental Health Inspector)
Discrimination
  Human Rights (Compliance/Human Relations Representative)

Issue Licenses

Licenses and Consumer Affairs (Licenses)
Construction and Land Use (Permits and Plans)

Provide Services

Legal
  Municipal Court
Housing
  Community Development (Housing and Neighborhood Development)
Information
  Fire
  Police
  Construction and Land Use
  Library
  Licenses
Health
  Health
Social Services
  Human Resources (Aging, Family and Youth, Community, Veterans)
Recreational Services
  Parks and Recreation (Recreation Programs)
  Arts Commission

Provide Protection

Physical Damage
  Police
Discrimination
  Municipal Court
  Human Rights
  Women's Rights

Figure 2.5. Departments and programs in a functional chart of a hypothetical city

Environment: Administration							
Section			Construction and Land Use				
Function	Fire Department	Police Department	Permits and Plans	Inspection	Plans Examination	Licenses	Library
Provide information	X	X	X		X	X	X
Safety inspection	X			X			
Taxes inspection						X	
Security inspection		X					
Housing & zoning				X			
Environmental standards					X		
Building codes				X			
Issue licenses			X			X	

Figure 2.6. Section/function cross-tabulation

when we match functions with the organizational structure can we identify the users who perform the functions that are relevant to a database. Figure 2.6 clearly illustrates this importance. The function "provide information" is a pertinent example. To figure out what departments in a city administration provide information, we would likely list the most obvious information agencies, such as the Library. However, when this function is checked against each structural unit, it is easy to discover that the Fire Department, the Police Department, and various programs in the Construction and Land Use Department provide information to the public as well, and on a regular basis.

Decomposition to Operation and User Types. The section/
function cross-tabulation can now guide the selection of types of
user. For each function we identify the job titles of persons who
are responsible for the function. To explore information needs
that are relevant to the function "safety inspection," for instance,
we need to talk to the head of the Engineering and Compliance
program in the Fire Department and someone at the Inspection
program, which is part of the Construction and Land Use Department.

Once we isolate each function and find the job titles that are
relevant to it, however, we can break down each function into
the individual operations, or activities, that are involved. The
function "Safety inspection" is composed of the following operations: collect data about a site, prepare background report, set a
visit, visit a site, make recommendations, and write a report.

Being able to look at each individual operation, rather than
each function, makes requirements collection more reliable because in this way the necessary level of detail can be gathered.
First, with a list of operations we can interrogate users in a sample
about specific activities. Rather than asking, say, a Fire Marshal
about the information he needs to inspect safety, we can provide
him with a list of the activities he performs for this purpose. The
Fire Marshal is then reminded of what is involved in carrying out
this function and can answer with great detail.

Second, stating explicitly the operations that constitute a function ensures that all the persons involved are considered. When
listing the persons who are responsible for safety inspection, for
example, we are not likely to include the department's secretary.
He is the one, however, who sets site visits. Having realized that
a secretary is among our potential users, and checking the other
operations for this function, we might find that he is also involved in collecting data about a site and in writing the final report.

Third, as we shall see later, to list the elements to be included
in a database we deal with data on the operations level. Using
the structure of an organization to help us in identifying these
operations *before* we analyze users' responses is a safeguard to
improve consistency and a great time saver.

Matching job titles with operations can be best done by constructing a user/operation cross-tabulation for each function, as illustrated in Figure 2.7.

One may argue that we could have analyzed the functions down to the most detailed level—even to the operations level—on the functional chart, and only then identified the type of users who perform each function. This approach is not practical, however. True, eventually we are interested in users themselves, and their department or program affiliation is not of any importance by itself; but we need to examine the organizational structure in order to "find" these users. In other words, we want to identify first the departments and programs that perform each function on the functional chart. Only then, when we further refine the functions, can we be guided to the relevant job titles (which are actually user types) that are involved in each function.

Constructing a functional chart of an organization, building a section/function cross-tabulation, and then a user/operation cross-tabulation constitute the major preparation for selecting a sample of users. User/operation cross-tabulations provide the

Environment: Administration				
Function: Safety Inspection				
User / **Operation**	Fire Marshal	Building Inspector	Secretary	Safety Specialist
Collect data about site	X	X	X	
Prepare background report	X	X		
Set a visit	X	X	X	
Visit a site	X	X		X
Make recommendations		X		X
Write a report	X	X	X	

Figure 2.7. User/operation cross-tabulation

types of user that need to be represented in a sample. Looking at the tabulation in Figure 2.7, for example, we know that we want to include in our sample at least a Fire Marshal, a Building Inspector, a Secretary, and a Safety Specialist. Other cross-tabulations will point to other types of user that need to be represented in a sample.

Readers may wonder if there are shorter and less expansive ways to get samples of users; while user/operation cross-tabulations are indeed a reliable reference to use when selecting users for a sample, constructing them requires much time. In practice, the answer to this question would depend on the resources available for the design of a database. We can safely say that, while there might be other methods to build a sample of users, this method is the most reliable. In addition, it simplifies future procedures and provides for easy consistency and quality checks. These features will become more apparent to the reader in the following chapters.

Our approach to building a sample of users for *un*structured environments further illustrates the importance of functions analysis for database design.

Sampling Unstructured Environments

For the purpose of our discussion, an unstructured environment is one in which the "picture" that users in the environment have of the enterprise has no clearly defined, or apparent, structure or routine. In contrast to city administrators, for example, who have a picture of Seattle that is strongly tied into the organizational structure of the city administration and to the routines followed in performing their daily activities, the picture that tourists and residents have of "what is going on" in Seattle is disorganized and somewhat chaotic. Obviously, there are broad categories of services, such as movies, restaurants, or museums, but there is no inherent structure within each category. Potential users have a variety of reasons for choosing a movie: some people may want to view it because the theater is air conditioned, others because they want to be entertained, and still others because they have to write a review about the movie.

To select a sample of users from the clientele environment,

which is an example of an unstructured environment, we impose a tentative "structure" on the environment. This structure is modified and refined as we collect data requirements and analyze them.

Because there is no structure to guide us, we use our commonsense and experience to determine (1) which functions are accomplished by users in the clientele environment, and (2) what are the typical subgroups of users in this environment. By picking our brains we come up with a list of functions that are performed by tourists and residents with relation to restaurants: going to a restaurant, dining in a restaurant, reviewing a restaurant, and running a restaurant. Using the same method we decide that tourists, residents, reviewers, and owners are the types of users who are involved with restaurants.

This list is our first approximation, and we need to represent it in a user/function cross-tabulation, as in Figure 2.1. From now on we are engaged in an iterative process to refine and modify users and functions in this cross-tabulation.

This iterative process implies that the sample of users and the set of functions may grow as design progresses. Such growth is bound to result in constant checking and rechecking of previous procedures. While we cannot avoid going back and forth as we progress in the design, we can reduce the number of such steps by being comprehensive and open-minded but at the same time rigorous and accurate.

When we construct our first approximation we can, for example, consult with various people, asking them what functions and types of users are involved. After an initial breakdown of types of users, we can approach a representative of each type and ask about the functions involved. Applying ideas thus collected, we may decide, say, that the function "Going to a restaurant" is better decomposed to three functions: "Getting information," "Making decisions," and "Getting there." We can also discover that waiters have been omitted from our initial cross-tabulation. Or, we may conclude that it is necessary to specify whether tourists come from the state, the country, or from abroad.

Because the breakdown of our environment to types of users is based on intuition, it is important to select representatives from all the subgroups of users within the relevant environment. If a database is geared to a certain population in the environment, say tourists, we want to include a relatively large number of tourists in our sample, hoping to collect the most comprehensive picture of their needs. Obviously, each function should be covered by at least one member of the sample of users. Thus we must have at least one owner in our sample because this is the only type of user who performs the function "Running a restaurant."

We should strive to have at least one representative from each function/user combination. Economic constraints, however, may force us to limit the types of users to be studied for each function. We may decide, for instance, to limit our questions about "Going to a restaurant" to tourists and residents only.

In addition, we need to be flexible in our selection. If, say, the one waiter we selected for an interview is not cooperative enough, another one can be located. If when talking to a waiter we find out that chefs of restaurants are also potential users, we should select at least one for our sample even if we did not plan to do so.

If, at some point during requirements collection, an issue emerges that requires special investigation, we should pursue the matter. Suppose, for instance, that after talking with most of our sample users we discover that tourists and residents would like to receive some information about a restaurant's chef. As designers of a new and sophisticated information source we need to know, as comprehensively as possible, which characteristics of chefs are important to users. Here we may proceed to select a new group of users, asking them a single question: What would you like to know about the chef of a restaurant to which you are planning to go? Asking only that specific question lets us interview a relatively large group and, therefore, develop a comprehensive list.

During requirements collection we can refine and modify types of users and functions. Analysis of the requirements collected will further enable us to break functions down into operations, as described in the next chapter.

These examples illustrate that being alert, exploratory, and open-minded while collecting requirements secures a comprehensive coverage of relevant user/function cells. Being rigorous and keeping the cross-tabulation structure provides for control over the data collected and is necessary for consistency.

REQUIREMENTS COLLECTION

Now that we have planned how to construct a sample of users, we are ready to consider the methods we can use to acquire information from potential users. In other words, we are ready to discuss methods for the actual collection of requirements.

To collect requirements from a sample of users, we can use most of the techniques used in field studies: questionnaires, interviews of potential users concerning their information needs, or observation of users as they perform functions pertinent to the database. The most useful methods are interviews and observations. While it is beyond the scope of this book to describe the practice of interviews or observations, a few issues are emphasized here.

A major concern is the nature of the questions to be asked in interviews. In contrast to data collection for surveys and similar studies, the purpose of interviews in requirements collection is to explore. Therefore, all the interviews with potential users should be open-ended: Users are asked questions to which they can respond in their own words at any length they deem appropriate, and they can include any information they feel is relevant.

Questions need to be open-ended for two reasons. First, whenever we ask a closed question we already assume something about the state of affairs. If we ask a person, for instance, on what days of the week he goes to restaurants, we are assuming that he has selected particular days for such an outing—which might not be true. Presumptions behind questions may not always be obvious. To avoid their implicit incorporation into our exploration it is better to ask an open-ended question, such as: When do you go to a restaurant?

Second, leaving the questions open-ended gives a respondent the opportunity to provide additional information that was not asked directly. Answering to the closed version of the previous question, the respondent might answer that he usually likes to go to a restaurant on Friday or Saturday nights. Answering the open-ended version he may add that he prefers to go to a restaurant that received a good review in the paper the same day, or that on rainy days he prefers to dine at home. At this early stage of the design we need as much data about the enterprise as we can collect. We want, therefore, to encourage users to provide us with all their thoughts and routines even if they are idiosyncratic.

Another major issue is how specific questions in interviews should be. People frequently associate open-ended requests with vagueness and fail to distinguish between the clarity of a request and its openness. Too many people remember being asked the vague question, "tell me about yourself." It is important to remember that while questions should be formulated in a manner that allows respondents to contribute information as they deem fit, requests for information should be clear and specific. They should address a particular aspect, function, or approach; and they should have a clearly defined subject. Thus, instead of asking a user to describe his habits that relate to dining out, we have to ask him specifically about when he goes to a restaurant, how he goes about selecting a restaurant, how he usually gets there, and so on.

Asking users general or vague questions has two undesirable results. First, a user may not remember to describe all the aspects and functions that relate to the question asked. For example, when asked about restaurant habits, a respondent may remember to explain when he goes to a restaurant but may not notice that the selection of a restaurant or the decision about how to get there relate to restaurant habits as well.

Second, posing a general question may lead users to perceive the database designer as either too lazy to formulate specific questions or ignorant concerning what information he really needs. Users deserve the designer's respect for their cooperation and practically speaking, they may not cooperate if they feel that the designer does not respect their effort.

The third major issue in interviews and observations concerns the attitude of the designer to user needs. It is not sufficient to require that a database designer be objective when collecting data. For this process to be successful, an interviewer or observer must be *genuinely* interested in the data that are being collected and *truly* nonjudgmental. Being uninterested or critical of user behavior is an attitude that would drive users away. In addition, the interviewer's or observer's personal values and habits about restaurants are not relevant to the study of the problem; they are important only if and when the interviewer is in the sample to be interrogated.

The last major issue is the explicit and complete recording of all interviews and observations. Because many decisions on the conceptual level are subjective, a designer must set a standard for data collection and follow it down to the smallest detail. A large amount of data has to be analyzed and given pieces of data must be found, often more than once. These are impossible tasks unless the data collected are organized in a unified manner. Interviews should be transcribed on special forms, and observations should be clearly reported regardless of the method used to record them in the field.

Figures 2.8 to 2.10 show forms that can be used for requirements collection. Each form is used for *one* function/user combi-

Requirements Collection Form	**Form Number:** 001
Environment: Clientele **Function:** Going to a restaurant **User:** Resident **Source:** Interview with Mr. S	**Page:** 1 **Version:** 1 **Date:** 8/8/85
I don't really like to eat out. My wife is a good cook, you know. But every once in a while we like to go to a real fancy place. I'm not picky about food, but French is my favorite—or maybe seafood. I use the Yellow Pages for restaurant telephone numbers to make reservations, but they don't tell you whether a restaurant is really good. . . .	

Figure 2.8. Transcription of the interview with Mr. S

nation. The form should first be given a title and then the environment that is being investigated, the function that is being described, the type of user that is questioned, and the person who is the source of information should be recorded. In addition, the designer should designate the form number for easy filing and retrieval of forms, the page number (some interviews or observations may be lengthy), the version number (there may be modifications), and the date.

All the forms in these figures have "Clientele" as their environment, and they describe the function of "Going to a restaurant." Figure 2.8 is a transcription of the answer given by Mr. S, a resident, concerning how he selects a restaurant. Ms. W is a tourist. Her response about her restaurant information needs is transcribed on the form in Figure 2.9. A resident, Mr. R, allowed an observer to spend a couple of evenings with him, observing his routine for going to a restaurant. Part of the observer's report is given in Figure 2.10.

SUMMARY

To collect user requirements, we study needs for each environment, one at a time, by eliciting opinions from potential users about their information requirements. The sample of users to be

Requirements Collection Form	Form Number: 002
Environment: Clientele	
Function: Going to a restaurant	**Page:** 1
User: Tourist	**Version:** 1
Source: Interview with Ms. W	**Date:** 9/9/85
When I want to go to a restaurant I want to know: what is the address; what is the price range; is it clean; what is their telephone number; do they take reservations; if not, how long is the wait; what is the house specialty; and things like that. . . .	

Figure 2.9. Transcription of the interview with Ms. W

Requirements Collection Form	Form Number: 003
Environment: Clientele **Function:** Going to a restaurant **User:** Resident **Source:** Observation, Mr. R	**Page:** 1 **Version:** 1 **Date:** 9/12/85

When Mr. R wants to go to a restaurant, he first decides what kind of food he would like to have. Then he looks in the Yellow Pages under the selected cuisine for a restaurant that is located on his bus route. When he finds a restaurant that satisfies his requirements, he consults the bus schedule. Three minutes before the bus is supposed to arrive, Mr. R puts his hat and coat on and leaves his house to go to the restaurant. . . .

Figure 2.10. Report of the observation of Mr. R

interrogated is selected by using cross-tabulations of users and functions for each subject area in an enterprise—one that designates for each function (e.g., Going to a restaurant, Dining in a restaurant) the types of users who are likely to perform it.

The approach to studying structured environments varies from the one we use to study unstructured environments. Structured environments guide us in defining the functions and users relevant to the enterprise. Through functions analyses of such environments we can find all the sections in an organization that perform a particular function. We can then further decompose each function to operations and user types.

Unstructured environments, with no apparent structure or organization, require structures to be imposed. Through a series of approximations, we can determine intuitively a structure that is likely to be hidden in each environment. As we collect and analyze data, we modify and refine this structure as needed.

The most common techniques for requirements collection are interviews and observations. Interviews should be open-ended and should include clear and specific questions. An interviewer or observer should be genuinely interested in the data and truly nonjudgmental. Data collected should be recorded as explicitly and as completely as possible on Requirements Collection Forms, which also record the environment, the function, the type of user, and the source of information.

REFERENCE

1. Martin J., and McClure, C. 1985. *Structured techniques for computing.* Englewood Cliffs, NJ: Prentice-Hall.

3

REQUIREMENTS ANALYSIS

Information recorded on the Requirements Collection forms needs to be organized in a useful manner into discrete "pieces" of data. Classification of sentences is the method to organize this information: Each sentence on the forms is analyzed to determine what piece of information it represents and which operation. A fact that places a restriction on an environment or on the enterprise, such as the legal age for drinking is considered a constraint. Depending on its nature, the information extracted from each sentence is then recorded in the Data Requirements, Operations Requirements, or Constraints forms. Each of these forms is a list of discrete sentences, each conveying information about a distinct element of data, a single operation, or a constraint. Inaccuracies may be introduced when users do not state requirements clearly, they state them incompletely, or with existing databases in mind. Being aware of these pitfalls and spotting them as they occur is a necessary step to control for accuracy.

The methods of collecting user requirements described in Chapter 2 involve practices that are by and large accepted in gen-

eral studies of user requirements and needs. For the collected requirements to be useful for database design, a specific method of
analysis is required. This method is explained in this chapter.

The Requirements Collection forms include a large amount of
data, but their organization is not directly relevant to the representation of data in a database. While each form includes information about requirements for a user/function combination, or
user/operation combination, what is needed for the design of a
database are discrete, well-defined, and distinguishable "pieces"
of data. For instance, we want to know if users in the clientele
environment are likely to ask for information about types of food
and, if they do, what exactly they mean by "type of food." In
the same fashion, we need to know if users in the administration
environment are likely to ask for information about the quality of
a restaurant, and how they define this feature.

Our task now is to collect the pieces of data that are scattered
in the various interviews and observation reports and organize
them in a useful manner. The procedure of organizing these
pieces of data is called *classification of sentences*, which involves
examining Requirements Collection forms one after the other and
analyzing each sentence in them. First, we analyze each sentence
on a linguistic level to eliminate implicit and ambiguous terms
and concepts. Then, we classify sentences by placing each in one
of three categories: the Data Requirements, the Operations Requirements, or the Constraints.

CLASSIFICATION OF SENTENCES

In linguistic analysis each sentence is scrutinized for comprehen-
sibility and ambiguity. If needed, the designer makes modifications so ideas are expressed clearly, even if that means contacting
a user again to ask about ambiguous phrasing. At the same time
control for synonyms and homonyms is exercised: Terms that
represent the same concept are merged so that one term is selected to represent the concept. Terms that represent more than
one concept (such as *bank, score*) are replaced by terms that represent the relevant concepts but do not express other concepts

(such as *shore, tally*). In addition, one looks for implicit elements—those that are only suggested and not plainly expressed—and rewrites a sentence to express them explicitly. Repetition and redundancy within each sentence is also reduced.

At this point a sentence is ready to be classified. Each sentence is examined to determine whether it expresses *data required to describe the enterprise,* or whether it expresses *how users act on data.* In the first case, a sentence belongs to the category of Data Requirements and, in the second, to the Operations Requirements. More explicitly, the Data Requirements Form is prepared to collect data about the enterprise (which is restaurants in our limited example), and the Operations Requirements Form to record actions that users take to perform the functions being analyzed. Examples of the Data Requirements and Operations Requirements forms are shown in Figures 3.1 and 3.2. Some sentences that do not belong to either the Data or Operations categories, in particular those that express *restrictions on the enterprise* or on an environment, are classified as Constraints sentences (Figure 3.3).

Forms of classified sentences are grouped by environment and function. In other words, for each category all the sentences that are extracted from one environment, and with relation to one function, are recorded on one form. A new form is selected for another environment/function configuration.

To obtain insight into the process of sentence classification, let us examine the interviews and observations reported in the Requirements Collection forms in Figures 2.8–2.10 and classify their sentences.

These forms show data collected from the clientele environment, which is an unstructured environment. As discussed earlier, for such environments the classification of sentences helps to define the operations—or individual activities—that are involved in each function. Moreover, the only reliable method for discovering these individual activities in an unstructured environment is through a systematic analysis of information provided by potential users themselves—an analysis such as the classification of sentences. Classifying sentences from the Requirements Collection forms for the administration environment, which is structured, would follow the same procedure. It is, however, somewhat simpler, because individual operations are already defined.

The Interview with Mr. S

The first sentence in the interview with Mr. S is: "I don't really like to eat out." We immediately notice that Mr. S uses *eating out* to mean the same thing as our prechosen term, *going to a restaurant*. To control for this synonym, then, we equate *eating out* with *going to a restaurant*. Now, some may claim that these are not real synonyms because what Mr. S means is that he does not like to eat in any place other than his own home, whether it is in a restaurant or at friends' houses. The second sentence ("My wife is a good cook, you know") only reinforces this explanation: The man likes his wife's cooking best.

From a database design point of view, however, we have to remember that we are not interested in the eating habits of Mr. S but rather in his routine concerning restaurants. Thus as far as we are concerned, the only place in which Mr. S eats out that is of interest is a restaurant. In other words, a restaurant is the only place that people eat out that is within our enterprise. We collect data about the enterprise of the database, and any information provided to us by users that does not relate to the enterprise is out of the scope of our investigation. Therefore, *eating out* and *going to a restaurant* are synonymous terms for the purpose of building this database.

Synonym Control. This example illustrates an important practice in database design: Control of synonyms is always exercised with respect to the database being constructed. Real synonyms, such as *customer's bill* and *customer's check*, should be controlled for as well as terms that normally would not be considered to be synonymous but that are synonyms from the enterprise's point of view.

The first sentence in its new form ("I don't like to go to restaurants") indicates an operation because it expresses an action that a user takes to perform a function: going to a restaurant. We can now list the first Operations sentence (which is numbered 01 in Figure 3.2): Go to a restaurant. Once we have identified a synonym, though, we need to record the equivalence in meaning for future reference. Therefore, the synonymous relationships should be recorded in the Operations Requirements Form together with the modified sentence itself (02): Eat out = Go to a restaurant. We may want to use our imagination here and speculate that some users may prefer the expression *dine out* and add this relationship as the third sentence in the Operations Requirements Form (03).

We should note here that, on the surface, the first sentence in Mr. S's interview does not provide new information since we have already identified the first operation as a function. This sentence is not a waste, however, because our analysis used it as a springboard to discover relevant information about operations—in particular, about the manner in which they are expressed.

Definitions. Examining this sentence further we can say that it actually identifies a restaurant as an "eating-out" place. This piece of information should not be neglected, and it clearly belongs to the Data Requirements Form because it relates to restaurants, which are part of the enterprise. One way to incorporate this notion is to formulate now a definition for a restaurant. We should know at this point that as we progress in the design project this definition is likely to be modified. But because we want to ensure that the eating-out aspect is part of a restaurant's definition, we can use it as a base for a preliminary definition.

To formulate a "good" definition takes experience in database design. At present, however, we should not be too concerned because any definition we formulate will still have to prove itself as a qualified definition in many succeeding stages. We can decide on a definition that seems most sensible to us at this stage of the design, but we have to be prepared to modify it later on to accommodate additional data and operations. Let us have, then, the following definition: A restaurant is a place where people who do not reside in it are served meals for a fee. This definition is sentence D1 in the Data Requirements Form (Figure 3.1).

The next sentence in Mr. S's interview, "my wife is a good cook, you know," is not within our enterprise and therefore, does not seem to contribute any information about data or operations requirements.

Mr. S's statement that once in a while he likes to go to a real fancy restaurant provides two items of data. First, he talks about the frequency with which he goes to restaurants. You may recall

Data Requirements Form		Page: 1	Date: 9/28/85
Environment: Clientele			**Form #**
D1	A restaurant is a place where people who do not reside in it are served meals for a fee		001
D2	Some restaurants are fancy		001
D3	Food has various types		001;003
D4	Food types can be characterized by cuisine or by main ingredient		001
D5	Restaurants have telephones		001
D6	Restaurants have reservation schedules		001
D7	The quality of a restaurant can be determined		001;002
D8	A restaurant has an address		002
D9	A restaurant has a price range		002
D10	A restaurant's level of cleanliness can be determined		002
D5*	Restaurants have telephone numbers		001;002
D6*	Some restaurants have reservation schedules		001;002
D11	The length of the wait in a restaurant can be determined		002
D12	Some restaurants have house specialties		002
D13	Some restaurants serve particular types of food		001;003
D14	Restaurants have locations		003
D15	Buses have routes		003
D16	A restaurant may be located on bus routes		003
D17	Buses have schedules		003

*A modified version of a previous sentence.

Figure 3.1. Data requirements form

that he does not like to go to restaurants but he does go every once in a while. Another way to express this notion is, I don't go to restaurants very frequently. From such a statement we learn that some people go to restaurants infrequently, an idea which suggests that others might go more frequently. We can formulate

Operations Requirements Form	Page: 1	Date: 9/28/85
Environment: Clientele		Form #
01 Go to a restaurant		001
02 Eat out = go to a restaurant		001
03 Dine out = go to a restaurant		001
04 Find restaurant's telephone number		001
05 Call restaurant to make reservation		001
06 Determine the quality of a restaurant		001
07 Decide what kind of food is desired		003
08 Select a restaurant		003
09 Consult bus schedule		003
010 Take bus to go to a restaurant		003
. . .		

Figure 3.2. Operations requirements form

this piece of data to be the next data sentence: The frequency of going to a restaurant varies from one person to another.

Looking at this new sentence, a critical designer may claim that it does not belong to the Data Requirements category because the data do not relate to the enterprise but rather to users. In other words, the sentence tells us something about people going to restaurants but nothing about restaurants themselves. This argument is valid; but even though it does not generate data that should be recorded on the Data Requirements Form, the sentence does provide an important piece of information. For example, when we finally operate the database we may want to provide one kind of display for frequent restaurant goers and another for people who go to restaurants only occasionally. In addition, by its nature, the sentence represents some restrictions on going to restaurants. It is, therefore, a good candidate for the Constraints Form, and it is recorded as sentence C1 in the Constraints Form (Figure 3.3).

Ambiguous Terms. The other element that stands out in the third sentence of Mr. S's testimony is the term *fancy*. From the sentence, it is clear that some restaurants are fancy and others are

Constraints Form	Page: 1	Date: 9/28/85
Environment: Clientele		**Form #**
C1 Frequency of going to restaurants varies from one person to another		001
C2 Some people are picky about food		001
C3 People have food preferences		001; 003
· · ·		

Figure 3.3. Constraints form

not. We can easily incorporate this piece of information into the Data Requirements Form, as we indeed do in this example, and add the next sentence (D2). But we should not make such decisions lightly. The term *fancy* is an ambiguous term. At best, it is relative: What seems a fancy place to one person may seem an ordinary restaurant to another. Therefore, we cannot introduce the word into our forms without further investigation.

We may take various approaches to clarify this ambiguous term. For example, we can go back to Mr. S and ask him directly to explain what he means by a fancy restaurant. Now, Mr. S may happen to be a very articulate and philosophically minded person, and he may indeed provide us with a succinct definition for fancy restaurants. Or, he might be too busy to think about the exact meaning of terms that everybody knows anyway.

But even if our new communication with Mr. S is successful, we do not have to accept his definition. True, he was the first person to mention this term, but when we record data about the enterprise we want to use definitions that would apply to a large variety of users. In short, there is no reason for us to use his definition just because he was the one who first used it. As a matter of fact, we are perfectly justified to conduct a short survey, for instance, among our friends to unravel what their notions about *fancy* are. In sum, we have to formulate a definition for the term and we can use any help we think is appropriate.

This term is a good example because it is a problematic one. It is likely that every person has a unique notion about fancy restaurants: They are highly decorated, complex, intricate, or of superior quality, to mention just a few attitudes. A database designer may decide to persist and find the "best" preliminary definition, thus eliminating ambiguity early in the design. Or, he may decide to leave the concept undefined until more data are collected so that Mr. S's expression can be compared with those of other users. The latter approach is taken here for illustrative purposes only.

In this stage of the design, we try to be creative and collect as many pieces of data as possible, whether or not they have been mentioned explicitly. We may want, therefore, to stop here for a moment and think about features that are special to fancy restaurants and that point to additional items of data. One suggestion that comes to mind is a dress code: Fancy restaurants may have dress codes. Whether we come up with this notion by ourselves or whether a user mentions the dress code feature, we need to check if there are restaurants with dress codes among those to be included in our database. In other words, if a piece of information suggests distinctions that we are not completely sure exist, we then must examine that part of the real world that is included in the enterprise to make a judgment about the distinction. Only then may we decide whether or not to include a piece of data in our database. In our example we decided not to include "dress code."

The next sentence, "I'm not picky about food, but French is my favorite—or maybe seafood," is also loaded with information. Here we have again a problem with an informal and relative term: *picky*. It is also a piece of data about users and should, therefore, be recorded in the Constraints Form (C2). As in the previous example, we decide to leave the ambiguous term undefined at this point.

Further advice that relates to the formulation of definitions is useful here. Whenever we are working on one portion of a database, we want to keep in mind that there are other portions that may be integrated with the current one later. The case of ambiguous terms is a pertinent example for the usefulness of this advice. Suppose we need to define the concept *a restaurant's level of cleanliness* (D10, described later) for the clientele. Here we may want to remember that administrators in the city are also interested in a restaurant's cleanliness, and whatever definition we use will have to apply to the whole database. Now, the city administration probably already has standards to determine whether or not a restaurant is clean enough. We could elect to use these standards for the definition of this concept in the Data Requirements Form for the clientele environment. After all, since tourists and residents do not have commonly accepted standards for what is considered to be a clean restaurant, we might as well use the administration's standards and provide for a smoother integration of the two portions.

The Specificity of Sentences. From Mr. S's statement that French food and seafood are his favorites, we can derive two notions. First, people have favorite foods, or, more explicitly, people have food preferences (C3). Second, French and seafood are types of foods. This immediately tells us that food has various types (D3). But it is also tells us that French and seafood are *particular* types of food.

Instinctively, we may want to generate a long list of sentences, such as: French food is a type of food, bar-b-que is a type of food, and so on. Upon examination, we can see that such sentences are much more specific than the previous sentences in the Data Requirements Form and deal with a greater level of detail. While there is a variety of food types, each sentence refers only to one type of food.

Although such sentences seem as factual in nature as the other sentences on the form, they are actually a *list* of types of food. They would correspond to a list of sentences such as: some restaurants are absolutely not fancy, some restaurants are not fancy, some restaurants are somewhat fancy, and so on. Obviously, such a detailed description would immediately generate an unmanageable number of sentences—a situation we would like to avoid. We can, however, incorporate the data we inferred from Mr. S's sentence by stating (D4) that types of food can be characterized by cuisine (as in French) or by main ingredients (as in seafood).

This example illustrates an important principle that, at present, is almost impossible to formulate in rigorous terms and sometimes difficult to follow in actual design: Sentences in the Data and Operations Requirements forms should neither be too specific nor too general. Each sentence must reflect *types* of "things" that we want to represent in the database rather than list *individual examples* of these "things." Later on, when we provide more rigorous definitions, we would state that such sentences should refer to entity types or attributes, rather than to individual entities or values.

Implicit Data. The last few sentences we have examined do not include information that is pertinent to Operations—they resulted in Data Requirements sentences only. The next sentence is more promising. Mr. S's statement that he uses the Yellow Pages for a restaurant's telephone number is implicit again because it only suggests an operation. If we formulate it explicitly, it tells us that one of the operations that is related to going to a restaurant is finding a restaurant's telephone number (04). It also obviously tells us that restaurants have telephones (D5). Within the same sentence Mr. S introduces yet another new notion: that one can make a reservation over the telephone. Such a revelation generates both an Operations and a Data sentence. The Operations sentence states: Call restaurant to make reservation (05), and the Data sentence mentions that restaurants have reservation schedules (D6).

On the surface, it looks as if Mr. S's complaint about the Yellow Pages ("they don't tell you whether a restaurant is really good") should be completely ignored because it mentions something that they "don't do," or a service that does not exist. We must try, however, to avoid the pitfall of that kind of rationale and remember that even though we are concerned here with data that relate to the enterprise, user requirements (in this case, to be able to find out whether a restaurant is good) should be collected even when they are not answered by current information systems. In fact, we want to be particularly alert and capture such requirements because they point to deficits or flaws in the information supply.

Thus, having the notion that somebody can tell somebody else whether or not a restaurant is good generates two observations. First, the quality of restaurants can be determined (D7); and second, one can, or should be able to, determine the quality of a restaurant (06).

Dealing with the notion of quality, we may go back and remember that Mr. S talked about restaurants being fancy. We may decide to compare sentences D2 and D7, and conclude that actually *fancy* means *of superior quality*. In this case the sentence about a restaurant being fancy (D2) is redundant because stating that the quality of a restaurant can be determined (D7) implies that some restaurants are of superior quality—that is, fancy (D2). If we accept a limited definition for *fancy*, we should integrate the sentences. While eliminating redundancy is a major task in our next step (the construction of the data and operations dictionaries), we are better off taking care of obvious cases of redundancy at this point in the classification of sentences.

The Answer of Ms. W

The answer given by Ms. W, a tourist, to the question regarding her information requirements about restaurants (see Figure 7.9) is quite explicit and requires only straightforward transcriptions of sentences. In addition, unlike the other users, she does not describe how she acts on data. This means that our chances to generate Operations sentences are quite slim. Going consecutively over Ms. W's requirements we can state that restaurants have an address (D8), restaurants have a price range (D9), and a restaurant's level of cleanliness can be determined (D10). Here again we may wonder if cleanliness is the same thing as quality in a restaurant. In fact, we may decide that we cannot go further before we explain explicitly what is meant by the "quality" of a restaurant. The flavor of such deliberations was introduced earlier with regard to the term *fancy* and we will not discuss the term *quality* here.

Redundancy among Sentences. Ms. W says she would like to know restaurants' telephone numbers and whether they take reservations. Here we may recall a previous entry concerning restaurants having telephones. We may not always be lucky and remember previous sentences. If not, we will record redundant information, with which we will deal in the next step. Here, however, we find immediately that D5 states a similar fact.

Examining the two similar sentences, we can see that there is no need to keep them as distinct pieces of information. The first sentence, however, mentions that restaurants have *telephones* while the second claims that they have *telephone numbers*. Obviously, we are not interested in the telephone as a physical object (its color, style, size, or ring) but as a communications device. Therefore, what is of relevance to our enterprise is the fact that the telephone has a number. We can rewrite sentence D5 in a modified form and eliminate the previous version. We also add the number of the Requirements Collection Form of Ms. W (002).

Ms. W's statement about reservations is another example of redundancy. Her notion about having reservations is expressed in a way that is somewhat different from the manner in which we previously recorded this fact. While we assumed that restaurants accept reservations when we stated that restaurants have reservation schedules (D6), Ms. W raised the idea that not all restaurants make reservations. Thus we modify the sentence D6 to express more precisely the reservation situation: Some restaurants have reservation schedules. Then we eliminate the old sentence.

Ms. W also made us aware that the length of the wait in a restaurant can be determined (D11), and that restaurants have house specialities (D12). Learning from our experience, we are more cautious here and state that *some* restaurants have house specialties.

Also note that the possible relationship between a restaurant's having a reservation schedule and the length of wait is irrelevant here. These are two discrete elements: Even if we can assume that such a relationship exists, we cannot find its regularity. In other words, if we know that a restaurant has (or does not have) a reservation schedule, we still cannot estimate the length of the wait. We might as well provide information about both elements.

The Observation of Mr. R

We turn now to the observation of Mr. R's preparations for dining out (see Figure 2.10). Since this text describes his routine when he goes to a restaurant, we expect to derive sentences in the Operations category from it.

The first sentence of this report informs us that Mr. R initially decides what kind of food he would like to have. This is an Operations sentence (07). In fact, we should have noted this operation earlier even though the concept of deciding "what you are going to have tonight" is not mentioned explicitly in any of the previous texts.

The first sentence also implies that food has various types (D3) and that people have food preferences (C3). If we happen to remember the placement of these sentences in our forms, we can just add the number of the Requirements Collection Form (003) to each entry.

The next sentence ("Then he looks in the Yellow Pages under the selected cuisine for a restaurant . . . ") brings up another important fact that we overlooked: A restaurant has a type of food. We should have spotted this idea earlier: When Mr. S claimed that he likes French food or seafood, he is implying that he would go to a restaurant that serves either French food or seafood. In other words, his selection of a restaurant is influenced by the type of food served there.

When we formulate a sentence to be added to the Data Requirements Form, we want to be cautious again and remember first that some restaurants may not serve a particular type of food, and second, that one restaurant may serve more than one such type. Therefore, we are safe in stating, Some restaurants serve particular types of food (D13).

Flexibility and Variability. From Mr. R's behavior we also learn that he looks for a restaurant not only by the type of food it serves but also by its location (whether or not it is located on his bus route). Much information is embedded in this simple statement.

First, we notice that restaurants are located somewhere, or that restaurants have locations. We may recall here that sentence D8 states that a restaurant has an address and thus conclude that adding a sentence about the location of a restaurant would be redundant. However, upon careful examination, we instead decide to consider the almost synonymous terms *location* and *address* as different concepts (for the time being).

The reason for this cautious step is that we may need to make a distinction between the physical place in which a restaurant is located (its *location*), and the "thing" that one has to put on a label to send an announcement to a restaurant (its *address*). Retaining the concept *location* enables us to designate explicitly the neighborhood or the name of the building in which a restaurant is located. It is possible that later on we will discover that this distinction is not relevant to the data in our database. Right now, however, we want to provide for maximum flexibility and to allow for a large amount of variability. We can now write the next sentence (D14): Restaurants have locations.

Next, we read in Mr. R's preparation that restaurants might be located on bus routes. To state this fact as a sentence in the Data Requirements Form, we first have to indicate that buses have routes (D15). Now we can transfer the text from the observation to add the sentence, A restaurant may be located on bus routes (D16).

The last sentence seemingly introduces a new constraint to our forms. Mr. R, unlike the other people from whom we have gotten information, prefers to go to a restaurant that is located on his bus route. Possibly we should add a constraint, such as some people select restaurants by bus route. This notion, however, is not really a constraint. The fact that Mr. R uses information about bus routes for his decision about a restaurant merely indicates that he needs to know the relationship between the location of a restaurant and bus routes, a connection indicated in sentence D16. He can then decide for himself what he wants to do with this information.

A more extreme example is the telephone number of a restaurant. One may argue that some people will not go to a restaurant before they call the place to make sure that it is open. It is obvious that we do not need to include this particular behavior as a constraint because the most important and the only relevant fact that can be derived from it is that the database should provide restaurants' telephone numbers. Users may then decide whether or not to call them, and what to ask when they do.

The next sentence, which is clearly an Operations sentence, generates Data Requirements and Operations Requirements sentences. When Mr. R finds the restaurant of his choice, he consults the bus schedule. Here again we have an example of a fact that we have missed. Mr. R selects the restaurant in which he is going to dine. This operation is almost always necessary for performing the function "Going to a restaurant." Yet, we managed to ignore it while analyzing previous interviews because no one else mentioned this particular action explicitly. Our next Operations sentence is, then, Select a restaurant (O8).

The other operation that should be recorded from this sentence is the fact that people consult bus schedules (O9). We cannot add such an Operations sentence, however, before we state that buses have schedules (D17).

The last two sentences in the observation of Mr. R's behavior add very little information. A single sentence is derived here: Take bus to go to a restaurant (O10). Mr. R's personal habits about timing and dressing for the event of dining out do not seem directly relevant to our database. We recommend, though, that these details be used to stimulate thought about additional facts and operations.

Now that we are familiar with data and operations requirements, we can summarize again the approaches to requirements collection and analysis. In particular, we can gain more insight into the difference between structured and unstructured environments.

You may recall that for unstructured environments we first developed a user/function cross-tabulation and then proceeded to interview, or observe, each type of user to identify data and operations requirements.

Structured environments, on the other hand, provided us with a more advanced starting point. Using the structure of organizations, we uncovered the *operations* involved and, at the same time, the user types that perform each operation. We then developed a focused list of user types, members of which should be interviewed or observed. We also had very specific questions to ask, or activities to observe, because for each user type we were interested primarily in the operations performed. Thus most of that ground has already been covered.

While for unstructured environments we studied the problem, uncovered data requirements, and identified operations requirements at the same time, for structured environments we can study the problem *first* by analyzing the organizational and functional structure of the organization. In addition, this analysis provides a tentative list of operations for the Operations Requirements Form. Then we are ready to gather individual data requirements, and to complete the list of the operations. Our path to recording data and operations requirements is more directed, since it can follow a systematic path and rechecking is limited to a minimum.

PITFALLS IN REQUIREMENTS ANALYSIS

When we collect data and operations requirements from users in unstructured environments, we assume reality is chaotic, with no apparent rules and regularities. We then prompt users to provide us with information about the enterprise, still in an unorganized fashion. Only then do we analyze the data collected so that we can present it in a systematic manner and eventually in a formal presentation. Because our initial data collection is performed in an unstructured environment, and because it relies primarily on information provided by potential users, we face three pitfalls: (1) requirements may not be stated clearly, (2) requirements may be stated incompletely, and (3) requirements may be stated in terms of existing databases. These problems can complicate the analysis of structured environments as well.

Requirements That Are Not Stated Clearly

Suppose we collect requirements by asking a group of selected residents a set of open-ended questions. One of the questions we ask is: To help us construct a database that provides information about restaurants, can you explain what kind of information you need from this database? We can expect a variety of answers, but one woman says that she would use the database when she feels like splurging. While she may know exactly what she feels or means, we do not know what information would be useful for her. Does she need a name of a "really good" restaurant? Does she want to know where the fancy restaurants are located? Does she need to know price ranges of restaurants? Or, does she need a mini-directory that points out the restaurants suitable for times one feels like splurging? This woman's statement, therefore, provides us with no data because it is not clear.

When we get an answer such as the one above, we are usually

alert enough to ask immediately, What would you be looking for when you feel like splurging? In this case the potential user is likely to clarify her response. Frequently, however, the ambiguity of an answer is not so apparent. Consider the following answer: "I would look for information about the easiest way to get to a restaurant from where I stay. For instance, what is the easiest way to get to the airport restaurant from downtown?"

During an interview this response could pass as specific and explicit. When we try to extract data from it, however, we soon find out that we cannot explicitly say what pieces of data are involved. We do not know what it is that the user has in mind when he is looking for the "easiest way." Is he thinking of the time it takes to get there, or is he looking for the shortest way? Is he going to drive his car, or is he considering public transportation? Is sitting comfortably in a bus easy enough, or would he rather consider a cab or a limousine? In short, we do not know which parameters the user employs when he judges what is the easiest way to get to the airport.

We can never make sure that all the responses of potential users to our requests are clear. We should try to remember, however, that some answers may seem specific and particular but still do not carry information in them. During interviews database designers should be alert to responses that appear straightforward and explicit but are really ambiguous or unclear.

Requirements That Are Stated Incompletely

Suppose we ask the woman who feels like splurging, "What would you be looking for?" She answers, "I want to go to a fancy restaurant." The response seems specific enough but we are still in the dark. We know the kind of restaurant she is interested in, but we do not know what she wants to know about this category of restaurants. Does she want to know whether there is a fancy restaurant in town? Does she want to know how to get there? Does she want to know the price range? There are many pieces of information that are associated with going to a fancy restaurant, and we need to know which ones are of interest to a potential database user.

We should remember that at this point we are not providing

information but instead are trying to identify what aspects, or elements of information, are relevant to potential users. When confronted with an incomplete answer, we can ask users to be more specific, or, better yet, we can ask them more specific questions. One could ask, "What would you like to know about a fancy restaurant? Are you looking for general information or do you need something specific before you can go to a restaurant?" Such questioning may elicit more information.

Most important, however, is to recognize immediately an incomplete answer that needs clarification. To ensure that answers are recorded completely, one should develop the habit of recording every minute detail, even when such details seem unimportant during interviews or observations. This habit often develops with experience or after a few "accidents." It can be acquired, however, by conscientious effort even during a designer's first attempt at constructing a database.

Requirements Stated in Terms of Existing Databases

Suppose the observer of Mr. R reports that Mr. R's favorite food is Indian. He saw him looking in the Yellow Pages for a restaurant that serves Indian food. From this report we conclude that some people select restaurants by type of food. We still do not know, though, why he looked for an Indian restaurant. The truth may be that Mr. R is looking for an inexpensive restaurant. Unfortunately, the Yellow Pages give no information about prices charged by restaurants. They classify restaurants by type of food, however. Mr. R, then, assumes that Indian restaurants are not too expensive and he looks for an Indian restaurant when he wants to eat out inexpensively. His searching behavior, or the information for which he is looking, is determined by the database that is available to him.

When an existing database cannot provide users with access to the information they need, most users try to manipulate it in various ways in an effort to get that information. Their answers to interview questions or their observed behavior frequently reflects what is available and not necessarily what is desired. This pitfall is a major obstruction to successful requirements collection. One should constantly look for this phenomenon, and for each response or piece of observation try to determine to what degree it is influenced by existing databases.

Fortunately, there are various ways to eliminate this obstruction, and some are quite effective. The most direct approach is to ask users to explain why they selected an Indian restaurant. As with incomplete answers, we can ask for further clarification to ascertain the source of a particular action or response. At times, however, a general "why" question is unproductive and more specific questions are required.

Consider, for instance, a person who states that she likes to go to Mediterranean restaurants. This term calls for special attention because Spanish, Italian, Greek, Turkish, Arabic, Israeli, Egyptian, and Moroccan food are all examples of Mediterranean cuisine. It is plausible to assume here that the user has selected this term because she saw it in the Yellow Pages. We may want to know exactly what interests our user. For that purpose, we ask her why she likes Mediterranean restaurants, or what she uses as the best feature of Mediterranean restaurants. Such questions will help us uncover properties of restaurants that are not listed in the Yellow Pages but that are relevant to potential users.

Eliciting information from people about their needs or about their perceptions of the real world is a task shared by a variety of professionals for a diversity of purposes. Thus, while no specific guidelines for requirements analysis have been developed yet, a designer could consult sources in other areas for useful methods to overcome these pitfalls.

A relevant example from the area of communications is the "sense making" approach that is being developed by Brenda Dervin [1]. The approach includes a theory and a set of derived methods for assessing how people construct sense of their worlds and how they use information and other resources in the process. The central model for analyzing states of information needs is called *situation-gap-use*. Here the information user is described as being in a particular situation that has been stopped because of some kind of gap. Once a bridge is built over the gap, the user makes use of whatever bridge is built.

Using this model in assessing the everyday information needs of citizens—and for a variety of other purposes, such as the improvement of information needs assessment during the reference interview in libraries—can be useful. Database designers would also benefit from using the situation-gap-use model. They can analyze operations described by potential users in interviews, or in observations, concerning the situation of the user, the gap, and the use a user would make, or has made, of the information. Such analysis would prompt the designer to ask potential users questions that elicit information that is important to the design of the database.

To create new and useful databases, designers often ask users to specify requirements or desired information that is not provided by existing databases. It seems, however, that posing such a general question to users is not particularly useful. When asked to list the data that are not available, users are most often likely to forget their unsuccessful attempts to get information from a database. More creativity is needed to elicit such information. A promising approach is to ask about information that users would get from sources other than databases. For example, one can ask a user to explain what questions she would ask a friend who has just tried a new restaurant, or what she would tell her co-workers the day after a visit to a good restaurant.

Unfortunately, there are no golden rules for avoiding these pitfalls in the collection of data requirements. It is vital, therefore, that we remain alert to such problems. Recognition of these obstructions when they occur may not eliminate them but it will save much time and frustration in the succeeding steps.

SUMMARY

Once the requirements are collected, we analyze each sentence on Requirements Collection forms. We first analyze for linguistic ambiguity: synonym and homonym control, expressing implicit notions in explicit language, and reducing repetition and redundancy within sentences. Then we classify each sentence as either a Data Requirements or Operations Requirements sentence, depending on whether it describes required data about the enterprise or whether it expresses how users act on data. Sentences that express restrictions on the enterprise or on an environment are Constraints sentences. The sentences are then recorded on Data Requirements, Operations Requirements, or Constraints forms.

Classification of sentences requires us to pay special attention to implicit data and to the "best" way to define a concept, as well as to the adequate treatment of ambiguous terms. In addition, we need to be consistent in the level of specificity in which we formulate sentences in the forms, try to eliminate redundancy among sentences as much as possible, and still provide for flexibility and variability.

The primary pitfalls in collecting data and operations requirements are (1) requirements may not be stated clearly because they are not specific or explicit enough, (2) requirements that are stated incompletely, and (3) requirements that are stated in terms of existing databases. Recognizing these pitfalls during requirements analysis is a necessary condition for successful analysis.

REFERENCE

1. Dervin, B., and Nilan, M., "Information Needs and Uses," in Williams, M. E. Ed. 1986. *Annual Review of Information Science and Technology*, vol. 21. White Plains, NY: Knowledge Industry.

4

DATA AND
OPERATIONS
DICTIONARIES

*The classified sentences in the Data Requirements, Operating Require-
ments, and Constraints forms still do not express explicitly enough each
element of data, an operation, or a constraint. In addition, there is likely
to be much redundancy and inconsistency among the sentences. The data
dictionary is intended to record each item of data (e.g., "restaurant,"
"type of food"), to define it, and to record relationships with other items
of data. Likewise, the operations dictionary is designed to record each
operation, such as "select a restaurant," and the items of data associated
with it.*

*Having to create entries for the data dictionary provides the first op-
portunity for a database designer to investigate thoroughly the nature of
each item of data and how it should be represented in the database. The
operations dictionary, at the same time, initiates the discovery of specific
associations among items of data—those that are relevant for the purpose
of a database. The data and operations dictionaries are the starting point
for a formal representation of data, which is the next process in the construction of the conceptual schema.*

As we analyze additional transcripts of interviews and observations, we record more and more sentences in the Data Requirements, Operations Requirements, and Constraints forms. In a short while we are likely to end up with a long list of sentences in each form—an abundance that may give us the feeling that things are somewhat out of control.

When we classify sentences we express each concept as explicitly as possible but we cannot spend much time on analyzing the contents of each sentence. During classification we are anxious to be as comprehensive and as flexible as possible. As a matter of course, we postpone decisions about problematic terms or concepts to a later stage when all the sentences are classified.

As we proceed, we also realize that there is redundancy among sentences, and possibly some inconsistencies. We try to deal with obvious cases during the classification procedure, those that clearly stand out (such as the difference between "telephone" and "telephone number"), but we leave more complex or problematic cases to the next stages of the design.

Once all the sentences are classified, the time has come to exercise some control over the sentences recorded in the forms. We need to put these sentences in order, and "take stock" of what we have recorded. For that purpose we build organized lists—or small databases, if you wish—in which we store information about data that are supposed to be stored in the city database, about the operations that are involved, and about the constraints encountered. Such lists are commonly called *dictionaries*.

The organized list of sentences retrieved from the Data Requirements forms creates the *data dictionary*. It stores data, or information, about data that are relevant to a database. The data dictionary is the heart of the conceptual schema. It defines the items of data included in a database, their relationships and the rules that must be followed for storage and retrieval of these data. This dictionary is continually revised and refined as the design process progresses.

The *operations dictionary* stores data about the operations that cumulatively constitute the functions under consideration. It is derived from the Operations Requirements forms. In it we explicitly define each operation and list the items of data that are necessary for its completion. The operations dictionary is used as the skeleton upon which we build the formal representation of items of data and their relationships.

The construction of the *constraints dictionary* is based on the Constraints forms. It is particularly important in verifying relationships and in checking the validity of rules.

While the operations and constraints dictionaries are used during the design of a database, they are later merged into the data dictionary. A working database has, therefore, only one dictionary: a data dictionary. It provides all the information about the data stored in a database and is modified according to changes introduced during the lifetime of the database.

THE DATA DICTIONARY

A data dictonary provides information about data that are stored in a database. Data dictionaries can take a variety of forms. Typically, a data dictionary is stored, manipulated, and maintained on a computer in the form of a database. Indeed, a number of software programs tailored for the construction and maintenance of data dictionaries are commercially available. Here, the dictionary is presented as a manual file in which the information about each item of data is recorded on a single card. A manual file may not be practical because it provides access only through one category (the CODE in our example), and because it can allocate only a limited space in which to record information. It is a good choice for demonstration, however, because it provides for direct, immediate, and simple recording and display of information.

Figure 4.1 is an example of the beginning of a data dictionary derived from the sentences recorded in the Data Requirements Form presented in Figure 3.1.

An entry in a data dictionary (or, a card in a data dictionary, in our example) includes a variety of features that relate to an item of data. In this chapter we examine the first set of features—those that derive from the Data Requirements forms. These features include the name, code, environment, description, source, synonym, and the subset-of features of an item of data.

The Name of an Item of Data

The first step in building a data dictionary is to list the items of data that are relevant to a database. To express these items of data, designers give a "name" to each sentence in the Data Requirements forms. This name captures what a sentence is "about" and thus brings to light an item of data. Sentence D12 in Figure 3.1, for example, is about "house specialties." In the entry for this item of data we can write, therefore, *house specialties* in the Name category (card 011 in Figure 4.1).

Naming each sentence is also necessary to eliminate redundancy among sentences. Consider, for instance, the two following sentences: "The length of the wait in a restaurant can be determined" (D11) and (D89, not listed in Figure 3.1): "Some restaurants are slow in seating customers." When screening, say, 600 sentences recorded in Data Requirements forms to eliminate redundancy, these two sentences may not seem alike.

The sentences are, however, about the same subject: how long one waits before being seated. More succinctly, they bring forth the same item of data: *wait* in a restaurant (or, *length of wait* in a restaurant—whatever we prefer to use). For the purposes of creating the database, then, these two sentences provide the same information and sentence D89 is redundant. Thus, by being forced to express the subject of each sentence, or what it is about, we can easily see which sentences are similar to one another. They can then be merged to express a single item of data.

In addition to redundancy elimination, a designer, must uncover relationships among items of data. Naming sentences usually facilitates a fluent and reliable detection of such relationships. The process of identifying relationships and their importance is examined in the succeeding section, "The Relationships Among Items of Data."

The Name category in the dictionary provides a name that can be used whenever it is necessary to refer to an item of data. Because names of items of data need to be stored in a database to be manipulated later on, they should be as short and succinct as possible. Thus we may prefer to use *being fancy* rather than *the degree of fanciness* because the former is shorter and more straightforward.

CODE <u>001</u>   NAME <u>Restaurant</u>   ENVIRONMENT <u>Clientele</u>

DESCRIPTION <u>A place where people who do not</u>
<u>reside in it are served meals for</u>
<u>a fee.</u>

SOURCE <u>D1</u>   SYNONYM ___   SUBSET OF ___

CODE <u>002</u>   NAME <u>Being fancy</u>   ENVIRONMENT <u>Clientele</u>

DESCRIPTION <u>Being expensive and possessing</u>
<u>uncommon qualities.</u>

SOURCE <u>D2</u>   SYNONYM <u>006</u>   SUBSET OF ___

CODE <u>003</u>   NAME <u>Type of food</u>   ENVIRONMENT <u>Clientele</u>

DESCRIPTION <u>The types of food a restaurant</u>
<u>claims to serve.</u>

SOURCE <u>D3,D4,D13</u>   SYNONYM ___   SUBSET OF ___

CODE <u>004</u>   NAME <u>Telephone</u>   ENVIRONMENT <u>Clientele</u>
<u>number</u>

DESCRIPTION <u>The number to call for information</u>
<u>and reservations.</u>

SOURCE <u>D5</u>   SYNONYM ___   SUBSET OF ___

CODE <u>005</u> NAME <u>Reservations</u> ENVIRONMENT <u>Clientele</u>
<u>schedule</u>

DESCRIPTION <u>A schedule that is used to reserve</u>
<u>a place at a certain time.</u>

SOURCE <u>D6</u>   SYNONYM ___   SUBSET OF ___

CODE <u>006</u>   NAME <u>Quality</u>   ENVIRONMENT <u>Clientele</u>

DESCRIPTION <u>The grade that is given by</u>
<u>reviewers.</u>

SOURCE <u>D7</u>   SYNONYM <u>002</u>   SUBSET OF ___

Figure 4.1. A data dictionary stored on cards

```
CODE 007       NAME Address       ENVIRONMENT Clientele

DESCRIPTION What is written on a mailing label
            when sending material to a certain
            establishment.

SOURCE D8           SYNONYM 012           SUBSET OF ___
```

```
CODE 008       NAME Price       ENVIRONMENT Clientele

DESCRIPTION The average price that is charged
            for providing commodities or
            services.

SOURCE D9           SYNONYM ___           SUBSET OF 002
```

```
CODE 009   NAME Cleanliness   ENVIRONMENT Cliente

DESCRIPTION The level of cleanliness in an
            establishment.

SOURCE D10          SYNONYM ___           SUBSET OF 006
```

```
CODE 010       NAME Wait       ENVIRONMENT Clientele

DESCRIPTION The length of wait for the
            provision of commodities or
            services.

SOURCE D11          SYNONYM ___           SUBSET OF ___
```

```
CODE 011       NAME House       ENVIRONMENT Cliente
                    specialties

DESCRIPTION Selected commodities or services
            in which an establishment
            specializes.

SOURCE D12          SYNONYM ___           SUBSET OF ___
```

```
CODE 012   NAME Location   ENVIRONMENT Clientele

DESCRIPTION The actual place where an
            establishment is located.

SOURCE D14          SYNONYM 007           SUBSET OF ___
```

Figure 4.1. (Continued)

In addition, it is desirable to use informative names. Using names that relate information about the item of data involved has two advantages. First, the more information included in a name the easier it is to distinguish one item from another. Second, by looking at a name, a designer can grasp what an item of data represents.

In some cases, however, it is difficult to find a name that is short and informative at the same time. In such a case, the designer should select a short name, even if it is not informative enough. The Description category should provide a fuller understanding of the subject matter involved.

The Code of an Item of Data

Codes provide for easy and fast reference from one entry to another, and also eliminate spending much time on searching for the "best" name for each item of data; they help avoid semantic problems.

As an illustration of the benefit of using codes, suppose we need to include information about the average price that is charged by each restaurant in the Seattle database. Suppose also that users would like to know the average price of each type of food, such as Chinese, bar-b-que, or vegetarian. In this case, the item of data *price of food* has two distinct interpretations: (1) the price charged in a restaurant, and (2) the average price of food of a particular type. We can name the first item *price of food in a restaurant* and the second *average price of food of a certain type*.

These names are obviously too long. We might then decide to use shorter versions that still indicate a distinction between the two, such as *price of food* and *average price of food*. These names, however, are not informative and may even be misleading.

First, the price of food in a restaurant is actually an average price (except for a few cases where restaurants charge a single price). Second, "average price of food" does not in any way suggest that type of food is involved. To know what these names represent, therefore, one would have to read the description of each item. Moreover, it seems that no matter what name is selected for these items of data, reference to the Description category is necessary. Thus we might as well give both items a shorter name: *price of food*. We can distinguish between them by having two cards in the data dictionary, with two different codes, one that provides information about food served in restaurants and the other about food of a certain type.

This example illustrates an important point. While names are informative, they introduce ambiguities because they are based on a live and natural language. Such ambiguities may prevent clear distinctions among items of data. Therefore, each item of data requires a code as well as a name. Only with codes can each item be identified *uniquely*.

Codes can be conveniently used to refer from one item of data to another. Suppose, for instance, we find it useful to designate on the card for *quality* that *being fancy* is a related concept. In fact, *quality* may have a host of other items of data to which it relates. To provide a unique identification of these items, we record their codes on the *quality* card, rather than their names. Codes are particularly suitable for this purpose because they are created to facilitate fast and easy access.

Unless required, codes can be coined independently of the meaning or name of the concept they represent and thus can be modified painlessly. While deliberations and further data may lead to a change in a name or any other category, rarely is there a need to modify a code. Suppose, for example, that a database designer decides at the last minute to change the name *being fancy* to *fanciness*. This change of name results in only one modification: a change in the Name category on the card for that item of data. The item *being fancy* may appear in entries for other items of data—such as *quality*—but no changes would be required there if *being fancy* is represented only by its code, which remains unchanged.

The Environment of an Item of Data

In addition to the name and code of an item of data, designers record the environment for which an item of data is recorded. It is important to record the environment under consideration because it may happen that items of data have the same name but require different descriptions in different environments. The telephone number of a restaurant, for instance, may refer in the clientele environment to the reservations number, but to the manager's number in the administration environment. Such discrepancies can best be discovered when the name of the environment is recorded.

The assignment of the Environment category is only temporary. Later on, when the schemata of individual environments are merged into one schema, this category will no longer be useful.

The Description of an Item of Data

An important category in data dictionaries is the description of the item of data. While names are informative enough for some items, many others require a description. The *price of food* is a clear case in point: Without a description, there is no way to tell what it represents. Moreover, having to write a description of an item gives a designer the opportunity to further analyze its meaning—and with more accuracy than previously possible before all sentences were classified.

Writing a description for an item of data is relatively straightforward for some items but requires exploration and brainstorming for others. The first sentence (D1) in the Data Requirements Form (see Figure 3.1) presents no apparent difficulties. The name of this item is *restaurant* and its description is actually given in the sentence itself. At this point, there is no reason to look for another. As we shall see, later on we will be required to re-examine this description and even introduce modifications.

Another example of a simple explanation is provided by sentence D5 (or its modified version, D5*). While it seems unnecessary to describe a telephone number, we need to be cautious and indicate that this item of data does not represent *any* telephone number but the one that is used for a specific purpose, when either calling for information or about reservations.

Several other sentences highlight items of data that can be described unambiguously: Sentence D6 suggests *reservations schedule*, and D8 brings up the notion of having an *address*. *Price, cleanliness, wait, house specialties,* and *location* can be similarly described straightforwardly.

Sentence D2, however, immediately presents a problem. Here we have to face the meaning of "being fancy" because we need to write a description. As in our last encounter with the concept, a few choices are available. We could just choose some kind of a description, knowing that it will be modified later on. We can even mark this description in some way to designate that it is incomplete and that it needs to be considered again.

To illustrate this option, we adapt this approach here and describe *being fancy* as being expensive and possessing uncommon qualities. Other options are discussed with the next examples.

We next examine sentence D3: "Food has various types." It is obviously about *type of food,* a concept that is seemingly clear and unambiguous. Trying to describe this item of data, however, we immediately encounter difficulty.

Suppose we need to explain the concept "type of food" to a person who spent all his life in a remote village in the mountains. Our best guess is to bring examples with us—of, say, French food, seafood, bar-b-que, and vegetarian. But we could never present all types of food, so the novice would not realize, for example, that sushi is a type of food, or that French seafood is one type of food rather than two.

Nor can we identify all the facets by which types of food are determined. We see that cuisine (French), ingredients (seafood, vegetarian), and method of cooking (bar-b-que) can determine types of food, but what facet characterizes "health food," "just desserts," or "homemade food"? And there might be other kinds of things that are considered to be types of food that do not occur to us when we explain the concept.

Every cook or restaurant owner can invent a type of food. An innovative chef may offer "energy food" for people who are involved in physical fitness, and yet another may specialize in "royal dishes" based on recipes used by chefs in the various European courts for the last three centuries. It might not be advisable, therefore, to try to predict all the various possibilities. We can agree, however, that most (if not all) restaurants, when asked, claim to serve food of a certain type. Thus *type of food* can be described as the types of food a restaurant claims to serve.

Our description of "type of food" is based on the assumption that most restaurants have this feature—they serve some types of food. That assumption clearly indicates something about the kind of food that is served, but we cannot describe this item of data on a general level that covers all possible types of food. Therefore, we leave the description open-ended and characterize it by what a restaurant claims is the type of food it serves.

The next sentence (D4: "Food types can be characterized by cuisine or by main ingredient") is again about *type of food*. It definitely should be recorded on the card for 003. Here we need to check how to modify the information already recorded on the card so it represents both sentences. The Code, Name, and Environment categories need no modification. We should, however, examine the Description category carefully.

We recall that when we decided on a loose description for *type of food* we considered the idea that types of food can be determined by cuisine or by main ingredients. Moreover, we found additional characteristics that can describe type of food. In other words, the data conveyed in sentence D4 was already considered by us and in fact the sentence does not add any new information. We can, therefore, leave the Description category unchanged. We do have an addition for the Source category, however. Sentence D4 should be added to the list of sources for this item of data.

Even though a designer usually analyzes sentences for a data dictionary in sequence, it is useful to look now at sentence D13: "Some restaurants serve particular types of food." This sentence is obviously about *type of food*, and, like the previous sentence, adds no information. In fact, the description we selected for this item of data implicitly predicts this sentence because it assumes that restaurants serve particular types of food. Here again we only list an additional source.

Another example of an item of data for which it is difficult to find an unambiguous description is the item *quality*, which is introduced by sentence D7 and is coded here 006. Again we encounter a knotty point because we need to define the quality of a restaurant. We can follow the example of *being fancy* and use a temporary description that will have to be changed later: "The degree to which food is delicious and the place is clean." Or, we could possibly use *type of food* as an example, and leave the matter completely unresolved by repeating the term in the description with no further elaboration. This latter option is actually a way to postpone the decision about a description, and by adopting it we may describe *quality* as "quality of a restaurant."

Another option, however, is to avoid an explicit explanation altogether but to describe how quality is determined. We can describe the quality of a restaurant as the grade that is given to it by reviewers. Taking this option, we assume that the different notions people have about the quality of restaurants follow from their application of different *standards* rather than different *interpretations* to the concept of quality.

This solution is sound because sooner or later we will have to indicate the quality of each restaurant about which we store information in the database. At some point we will have to decide how to determine quality and who are the "authorities" to make such judgments. Suppose we decide to use a panel of judges to determine the quality of each restaurant. As a result, we receive several quality assessments for each restaurant, each of which differs from the others. In our example we elected to use restaurant reviewers as panel judges. We made this selection in the early phases of data dictionary construction, hoping that reviewers would be more consistent in their judgment than others selected arbitrarily.

More generally, we conclude that when an item of data represents a subjective or unstable feature, designers note in the Description category how information about the item could be collected without describing the item itself. To record information about such items in a database, some decision needs to be made about its representation. Designers can select this option at this early stage of the construction of a data dictionary *only if* they are ready to consider representations of items of data.

It should be noted that the decision made here to qualify reviewers as authoritative judges may be premature. At this point, however, it seems attractive for two reasons. First, it is general enough and can also apply to, say, movies, libraries, or concerts. Second, it is open-ended enough because we have not defined as yet who qualifies as a reviewer. Later on, when we know more about the requirements of the database, and when the time comes to generate rules, we can select reviewers who answer those requirements.

This approach could also have been applied to the case of *being fancy*. Instead of choosing a description that is subject to later change, we could decide that there is no objective way to describe the concept *being fancy*. We might as well agree that we do not know what *being fancy* actually means; still, it is a common term and people usually can tell whether or not a restaurant is fancy. Thus, instead of describing this feature, we can establish a committee that decides for each restaurant whether or not it is fancy. The description of this item of data would then be, An attribute that is assigned to a restaurant by the Fancy Committee.

Such an approach is not suitable for the description of *being fancy*, though. First, an average city does not have a Fancy Committee, and it is not clear whether city administration would agree to appoint and support such a committee when its sole purpose is to provide information to a database. Second, unlike the feature *quality*, which needs to be determined by a large variety of attributes—such as the service, the view, or whether or not it is roomy enough—we can assume that eventually we can come up with a description of the feature *being fancy* that would satisfy most users of a database. It makes more sense, therefore, to attempt a first approximation of such a description in this early stage of data dictionary construction.

On a general level, we conclude that in instances where, given enough information, designers can find a satisfactory description for an item of data, they should provide a temporary description they know is incomplete. Designers, in other words, choose to start with a partial description, while recognizing that as they collect more information the more likely they are to arrive at a well-defined description.

Similarly, we could have compiled a list of types of food (which would have to be constantly updated) and describe *type of food* as the items from that list that best describe the food that is served in a restaurant. One can immediately see that such an option results in many complications. First, we would have to explain clearly what is meant by "best describes type of food." Second, we would have to decide how it is to be determined, whether by yet another committee, restaurant owners, or by another "expert." Third, no list of types of food is actually available. Even though we may need such a list if the variety in food types is overwhelming, its necessity is not yet obvious. We are much better off to postpone the decision about an informative description of this item of data.

On a general level, we conclude that designers may repeat the name of an item of data in the description without adding much information when it is unlikely that they will come up with a clear-cut description of the item. Additional information may shed more light on the usage of the item of data, and its description may be accordingly changed later on.

Last, in screening the various sentences in the Description category, one finds no mention of restaurants, except for two items of data (*restaurant* and *type of food*). This dearth may seem peculiar since our main interest is restaurants, but no omission has been made. Even though we are now developing the restaurant section of the Seattle database, we need to keep in mind that eventually this section will be merged with other sections. Most items of data we record here apply to other events or services as well. Thus instead of limiting our descriptions (and names) to specifically bound terms, such as *price of food*, we are much better off to use a more general name, such as *price*, and to describe the item in a manner that would apply to other items of data.

General descriptions provide for a smoother merger with other sections of the database. Instead of merging the cards for *address of a restaurant, address of a museum, address of a movie theater,* and so on, we already have a card that represents this item in a manner that is applicable to museums or movie theaters. We need only to check whether any modifications are required.

One should be cautious, however, and avoid describing an item in terms that are too general to be informative. The item *telephone number* is an example of such a pitfall. In their attempts to use general descriptions, database designers may decide to describe a telephone number as "the number at which to call an establishment." An establishment may have several telephone numbers, however, each used for a different purpose. As explained before, this distinction should be made clear at the outset because the database is designed to serve each and every purpose. Therefore, the description listed in Figure 4.1 ("The number to call for information and reservations") is general and specific at the same time: It does not refer to a specific establishment but it does spell out the service that is provided when a telephone call is answered.

The Source of an Item of Data

It is important to include in a data dictionary the source from which an item of data has been derived. Knowing the source enables database designers to trace back the way an item evolved.

As more information is collected about items of data, designers must be more rigorous about descriptions and definitions of items to be stored in the database. In some cases they may need to examine the original interview or observation report to support a sound and helpful decision. A designer may be required to decide once and for all whether or not, for instance, *address* and *location* can be entered as two distinct items of data; to do so, she studies the instances where these terms were mentioned by users to find out if they were used interchangeably.

When items of data are derived from Data Requirements forms the number of the sentences from which each item was derived should be recorded. As illustrated by previous examples, an item of data can be derived from more than one sentence—as is *type of food* (003), which is derived from three sentences.

The Relationships among Items of Data

Some sentences point to items of data that are different yet related in a manner that is independent of a particular database or of a specific environment. Such relationships frequently prove to be significant in later stages of the design and even when searching an operating database.

The first of such relationships is recorded in the Synonym category. This category is necessary for instances where two items of data are similar to one another. In some cases the items bound by this relationship might be so similar to one another that designers decide later on to merge them into one item.

The item *quality* is an example of a piece of data that is similar to another but is unlikely to be merged with it. The term related most closely to *quality* is *being fancy*, because fancy restaurants are usually considered to be of high quality.

Now, some restaurant goers would not agree with this assumption: Some fancy restaurants, they may claim, are not that good.

Others may consider the two concepts to be synonymous. Obviously, we encounter here a subjective judgment, but we can see clearly that the two concepts are strongly related. We also know that we need to keep them as two distinct terms because we have not yet decided about their final description. Later on we will have to make a decision whether or not these terms are identical for the purpose of our database. Therefore, we designate *being fancy*, which is coded 002, as a synonym on the *quality* card, and reciprocate by designating *quality* as a synonym on the card for *being fancy*.

Another example, and a more obvious one, is demonstrated by the similarity between the items *address* and *location*. Unlike *quality* and *being fancy*, these two concepts are probably used interchangeably by most people. Earlier, however, we decided to keep these two as distinct items as a precautionary measure. Obviously, therefore, we need to indicate that one item is synonymous with the other.

The other category recording significant relationships is Subset of. In this category designers list the codes for other items that *include* that specific item of data.

A simple example is provided by the items *being fancy* (002) and *price* (008). The description of the former, you may recall, includes the feature "being expensive." Price is, therefore, included in the determination of whether or not a restaurant is fancy. Or, the item *price* is a subset of the item *being fancy*. We record this relationship on the card for *price*, as shown in Figure 4.1.

A less obvious example is the relationship between *cleanliness* and *quality* (or *being fancy* for that matter). For a restaurant database, these items are likely to be considered as two distinct items. After all, restaurant reviewers report how good the food in a restaurant is as well as how clean it is. It stands to reason, therefore, that users would probably ask about both of these two features of a restaurant.

On the other hand, the quality of a restaurant is also determined by its cleanliness. When a person tells us about going to a really good restaurant, we assume that the food was delicious, but we also infer that the place was clean (even if we do not think about it at the time). It seems, therefore, that *cleanliness* is a subset of *quality* because the former is one of the features that determine the latter.

We should be reminded here that we still do not have a definite description for the item *quality*. A conclusive decision about the matter has been postponed to a later stage in the design. It is clear now that the postponement is useful: Once we uncover the relationships between this concept, or item of data, and the other items to be included in a database, we are more likely to come up with a stable and useful description for the concept. Once a more definite decision about the description of *quality* is made, the features that are considered to determine it will be explicitly stated, and some of these features are already recorded as distinct items in the database.

Realizing the importance of uncovering such relationships among items of data is crucial to the success of a database. In addition to the impact on the conceptual schema, we can easily see how such relationships can be used when data are retrieved from an operating database. Suppose a user wants to know how good the Minaret restaurant is. Searching our city database, she discovers to her dismay that no review has been published about it, and therefore, she has no data about the *quality* of the restaurant. If the city database can then display all the other categories that relate to the quality of a restaurant, she would find *cleanliness* as a subset of quality. She then searches for information about the restaurant in the *cleanliness* feature and discovers that such information is available, for every restaurant in the database, because city administrators make their ratings available to the public through our database. Here, we are better off when we can at least inform the user that the Minaret restaurant is immaculate, even though we still do not have information about other aspects of its quality.

There is no quick and easy method for discovering synonym and subset-of relationships. Each item of data when first recorded needs to be checked against the items already in a data dictionary for possible relationships. Some help is provided, however, by software for the construction of data dictionaries. Some software programs enable a database designer to generate a KWIC (Key Word In Context) index, which displays each meaningful word in the Description category. Using such an index, a designer can compare items that have identical words in their descriptions to determine whether or not they relate to one another. While it is a useful aid to the discovery of relationships among items of data, a KWIC index cannot substitute for a constant check of individual items. The examples discussed above clearly demonstrate this notion: *being fancy* and *quality* have no common words in their descriptions, nor do *cleanliness* and *quality* or *address* and *location*.

The Synonym and Subset-of categories are construed here as universal relationships in the sense that they are independent of a particular database and a specific environment. They represent relationships that always exist among items of data, or concepts. These are, therefore, similar to relationships that exist among concepts in an index language. Thus the approach to uncovering these relationships and to their maintenance should follow procedures that have been proven to be useful in the construction of index languages.

THE OPERATIONS DICTIONARY

The operations dictionary stores data about the operations that cumulatively constitute the functions under consideration; it is a tool to keep stock of the activities for which a database is going to be consulted. Such activities, which are called operations, are collected from Requirements Collection forms and recorded on Operations Requirements forms (see Figure 3.2). The sentences in the Operations Requirements forms, however, are listed in the order in which they have been recorded and no attempt to organize them in a useful manner was exercised when the requirements were first collected.

To construct an operations dictionary, designers organize these sentences to represent distinct operations and they analyze them to identify the items of data that are involved in each operation. Similarly to items of data in a data dictionary, we name each operation, assign it a code, provide a description, and record the source from which it has been derived. The additional category, Data Involved, is central to the construction of the conceptual schema. It represents the first attempt to describe how items of data relate to one another in a particular database and for a specific environment (Figure 4.2).

The selection of names, codes, and descriptions for operations is very similar to the processes applied in the construction of data dictionaries: The code includes an additional letter to distinguish between items of data and operations; the name should be as short and succinct as possible; the description should provide a more detailed discussion of the operation than the name implies; and the source refers to the number of the sentence in the Operations Requirements Form.

Control over redundancy is facilitated by the Name category, but also by some sentences in the Operations Requirements Form. Sentences 02 and 03, for example, do not represent a distinct operation but rather alert the designer to synonymous terms that might be used in other sentences.

The category Data Involved is provided so a designer can list all the items of data that are involved in accomplishing an operation. For each operation we consecutively examine each item of data in the data dictionary (see Figure 4.1) to determine whether or not it is involved in the operation. One should be creative when selecting the items that are involved, and try to uncover relationships that might not be apparent at first sight. In short, we should attempt to be as exhaustive as possible in assigning the items that are involved.

Some operations are limited in their scope and the items of data that are involved in accomplishing them can be directly derived from their description. The operation *find telephone number* (P001) is an example of such an operation. Its description refers us to three items of data: *restaurant, telephone number,* and *directory* (which is not listed in Figure 4.1 but added here for illustration).

Other operations require more examination and investigation. The operation *find out about quality* (P003) is a clear case in point. From the information recorded on the card for *quality* in the data dictionary, it is clear that *being fancy* and *cleanliness,* as well as *quality,* are involved in determining how good a restaurant is because users take these items into consideration in determining the quality of a restaurant.

				DATA INVOLVED	
CODE	NAME	DESCRIPTION	SOURCE	CODE	NAME
P001	Find telephone number	Consult a directory to find restaurant's telephone number	04	001 004 017	Restaurant Telephone # Directory
P002	Make reservation	Contact restaurant to make reservation for a certain time and space	05	001 004 005	Restaurant Telephone # Reservation schedule
P003	Find out about quality	Find out how ''good'' is a restaurant	06	001 002 006 009 035 037	Restaurant Being fancy Quality Cleanliness Reviewer Grade
P004	Select type of food	Consult a directory to identify type of food that is desired	07	001 003 017	Restaurant Type of food Directory
P005	Select a restaurant	Consult a directory to identify desired restaurant	08	001 017	Restaurant Directory
P006	Consult bus schedule	Consult bus schedule to find bus route and times of departures and arrivals	09	021 022	Bus Bus schedule
P007	Take bus	Take bus at a certain time and place to go to restaurant	010	001 012 021 022	Restaurant Location Bus Bus schedule

Figure 4.2. The operations dictionary

The description of *quality* in the data dictionary, however, is based on a grade that is given to a restaurant. Suppose that *reviewer* and *grade* (which is the grade given to a restaurant by a reviewer) are also items in the data dictionary. Even if it is not clear at this point how the grade for *quality* is assigned, these two additional items should be included in the operation *find out about quality*. The reason is simple: Some users may find out about quality by reading, say, a restaurant review in the newspaper. The grade given by a reviewer to a restaurant, therefore, is definitely a factor that is involved in finding out about the quality of a restaurant. Thus, they should be included in the Data Involved catetory.

The operation *select type of food* also exemplifies the need for creative thinking when assigning items to operations. While its description involves only two items of data, *type of food* and *directory*, the description of the item *type of food* (003) is bound to a restaurant. Since *type of food* can be introduced only if a restaurant claims to serve it, the concept *type of food* is always related to the concept *restaurant*. We can say that an expanded description of this operation may be, Consult a directory to identify type of food (that is claimed to be served by a restaurant) that is desired. The item of data *restaurant* is, therefore, involved in this operation.

One should note that the item of data *restaurant* is involved in most of the operations that are recorded in the example. This is not surprising: "Going to a restaurant" is the function that we are analyzing for this example. Restaurants, in other words, are central in some sense to all the operations involved in this function.

One should not assume, however, that *restaurant* would necessarily be involved in *all* the operations here. The operation *consult bus schedule* (P006), for instance, does not involve *restaurant* because it is limited to acquiring information about route and departure or arrival times of a bus—activities independent of restaurants. The next operation, however, *take bus* (P007), makes the connection between these items of data because it describes the activity of taking a bus to a restaurant.

The operations dictionary establishes the connections among items of data that are relevant to a particular database and a specific environment. Once these connections are represented in the conceptual schema (in the form of relationships), this dictionary is needed only for additional checks. Unlike the data dictionary, which is modified and maintained during the lifetime of a database, the operations dictionary is used only as a tool to establish relationships. It is important, therefore, to be extremely cautious in its construction. In particular, it is essential to check and recheck the Data Involved category for omissions.

THE CONSTRAINTS DICTIONARY

In a manner similar to the way the data and operations dictionaries are built the constraints dictionary is constructed to organize and control the constraints on the data to be stored in a database (Figure 4.3). The operations and constraints dictionaries have in common the Name, Code, Description, Source, and Data Involved categories. The constraints dictionary has, in addition, an Operations Involved category. The Involved categories are designed to record the items of data and the operations for which a particular constraint is relevant. Thus the constraint *picky* (N002) should be considered when decisions about *restaurant, type of food, quality,* and *cleanliness* are made, as well as when one considers the operations *find out about quality* and *select type of food.*

The constraints dictionary is consulted during the whole process of database design. Decisions on all levels should conform with the constraints listed. It is advisable, therefore, to routinely check the dictionary at the end of each phase of the design, even if the dictionary has been consulted throughout that phase. In particular, it is important to consult the dictionary when rules are formulated (see Chapter 7) and during the evaluation of the conceptual schema (see Chapter 8).

SUMMARY

The first process in building the conceptual schema, the *study of the problem,* culminates in the construction of the data and operations dictionaries.

CODE	NAME	DESCRIPTION	SOURCE	DATA INVOLVED		OPERATIONS INVOLVED	
				CODE	NAME	CODE	NAME
N001	Fre-quency	Frequency of going to res-taurant varies from one person to another	C1	001	Restaurant		
N002	Picky	Some people are picky about food	C2	001 003 006 009	Restaurant Type of food Quality Cleanliness	P003 P005	Find out about quality Select type of food

Figure 4.3. The constraints dictionary

The data dictionary organizes and controls the data that is stored in a database. It is the heart of the conceptual schema, and, in fact, of the database itself because it includes information about the data to be stored. While the first steps of its construction are based primarily on the information recorded in the Data Requirements forms, subsequent procedures involve explorations of additional sources. As a result, new categories will be added to each entry and the content of existing ones might be modified.

Each sentence in the Data Requirements forms is analyzed to identify its subject matter. The subject, in turn, reveals an item of data whose name and code create an entry in the dictionary. Organizing these sentences in a data dictionary provides for detection of redundancy and inconsistency among sentences.

The entry for each item includes, in addition to the name and code, the name of the environment for which the item was discovered, a description of the item, a record of its source, and references to other items of data that are synonymous or that include the item.

The description of some items of data may require complex decisions. One group of such items cannot be described straightforwardly at initial stages; a satisfactory description must await the gathering of enough information. For this group a designer may provide temporary descriptions that are incomplete, knowing they will have to be revised later on. The descriptions of such items develop as the database design progresses.

The second group includes items for which it is clear a designer has little chance of coming up with a clear-cut descripton. Additional information, however, would shed more light on their usage. Here the selected option is to postpone the decision about the items' descriptions to the point where additional information is no longer useful.

Items of data that present subjective or unstable features define the third group. For them, a designer may want to describe how information could be collected to be stored in a database, without describing the items themselves at all.

The synonymous and the inclusion (subset-of) relationships among items of data are determined independently of a particular database or of a specific environment. They are defined when two or more items of data are very similar to one another or when one or more items of data fall under another item. Noting these relationships is important both to the construction of a database and to its use.

An operations dictionary stores data about the operations that constitute the functions under consideration. As are items of data in the data dictionary, each entry in this dictionary is identified by a code and a name. A description of an operation and the source from which it is derived follow.

The operations dictionary establishes for the first time relationships among items of data that are distinct for a particular database and a specific environment. To facilitate the expression of such relationships, all the items of data that are involved in accomplishing each operation are listed in the operation's entry. It is important to attempt a comprehensive list of items for each operation to ensure that no relationship that needs to be expressed in a database is omitted.

The data and operations dictionaries prepare the ground for the next process in the construction of the conceptual schema: formal representation of data.

5

THE ENTITY-
RELATIONSHIP
MODEL

*Once the data and operations dictionaries are established, it is time for
the formal representation of the database's enterprise. The Entity-
Relationship Model is a tool for such representations. It consists of three
fundamental concepts: entity, relationship, and attribute. The construction of an Entity-Relationship Diagram is based on the operations dictionary: Each entry in the dictionary represents a relationship between
entities—a relationship that is represented in a mini-diagram.*

*When the next entry is analyzed, the mini-diagram that it creates is
integrated with the mini-diagram created for previous entries. When all
the entries in the operations dictionary are represented, the first version
of the Entity-Relationship Diagram for the relevant function is completed. To perform this transformation from a list of discrete entries to
an integrated diagram, designers use their knowledge concerning relationships among entities and their capacity to distinguish between entities and attributes.*

To construct data and operations dictionaries, database designers collect information about habits and needs of potential

users, as described in the previous chapters. Designers first receive comprehensive descriptions of actions that people take to perform a function—"going to a restaurant" in our example. They then factor these descriptions into individual items of data and operations. While they keep in mind the database as a whole, the treatment of items of data and operations requires that each item and each operation be isolated from the others.

To study the problem, designers examine closely, and in isolation, each of the elements that is involved in a function. They decompose a function into its elemental components. For each such component, a designer develops an entry in the data or operations dictionary, describes it, and records its general relations to other components in the dictionaries. Once this procedure is accomplished for all components, it is time to assemble them together to represent the original function in a formal model.

The Entity-Relationship Model has been gaining recognition as being suitable for the expression of items of data and their relationships that are specific to a database. This model was first introduced in 1976 by Peter Pin-Shan Chen [1] and has since attracted much attention, resulting in further developments and enrichments of the model. The model facilitates a graphical representation of the components of a conceptual schema, which is called the Entity-Relationship Diagram. With this diagram, the network of relationships among items of data can be clearly and explicitly expressed.

ENTITIES

An *entity* is a "thing" that can be distinctly identified. Any distinguishable object, real or abstract, that is to be represented in a database is an entity. Thus the Minaret restaurant, bus number 43, the PauPau restaurant, the telephone number 325–7295, the restaurant reviewer Mr. Smith, and Mexican food are all entities that will be represented in the Seattle database.

When developing a conceptual schema, however, designers are not interested in individual entities but rather in types, or sets, of entities—such as restaurants, buses, telephone numbers, reviewers, or types of food. Therefore, we look at *entity types*, which are sets of entities, rather than examining individual entities.

Looking at our data dictionary (see Figure 4.1) we can see that we have already established the entity types that are of relevance to the city database because each item of data can represent an entity type. When we constructed the data dictionary, however, we were not concerned with individual entities, nor with the concept of entity types—we derived items of data from sentences that were general in nature. Now that we have to consider which entity types to include in the formal representation, we can be more rigorous about our definitions. We must examine what constitutes an entity and what is an entity type.

Most items of data, such as *restaurant, address, price,* or *house specialties,* are clearly entity types rather than individual entities. Sometimes, however, what constitutes an entity type is unclear, and further examination of individual entities becomes necessary. Suppose that a data dictionary that relates to restaurants includes items of data such as *live music, valet parking,* and *birthday parties for kids.* Is each of these items an entity type, like *type of food* or *house specialties,* or are they instead individual entities that together form an entity type—say, *special services?*

The answer to the question depends on design specifications for a database. *Live music,* for example, should be considered an *entity type* if the city database is designed to include the name of each group that is performing in each restaurant, or even when the designer decides to provide information about the type of music that is performed in a restaurant, such as western, country, or baroque. In this case, each group of musicians—or each type of music—is an individual entity, and the set of all the groups—or of all types of music—is an entity type that is called *live music.*

On the other hand, if the city database is not intended to be so specific and detailed, *live music* is but one of the entities that together form the entity type *special services.* Here an operating database only informs users whether or not a restaurant has live music, but no information about its nature or performers is stored.

While it is very important to distinguish between the concepts *entity* and *entity type,* in our discussion here we will use the term *entity* to designate *entity type;* accuracy will be sacrificed for the sake of simplicity. In discussing the conceptual schema, we almost always refer to *entity types* and only rarely to individual *entities*. Therefore, in the following, *entity* means *entity type*, and when individual entities are discussed a special mention is made.

In the Entity-Relationship Diagram, entities are represented by rectangular-shaped boxes, as illustrated in Figure 5.1.

RELATIONSHIPS

A relationship is an association among entities. For example, "is located in" is a relationship between the entities *restaurant* and *location*, and "goes to" is a relationship between the entities *bus* and *location*. In the Entity-Relationship Diagram, relationships are represented in diamond-shaped boxes (see Figure 5.1).

With these two fundamental concepts of entity and relationship we are ready to start constructing the Entity-Relationship Diagram for the function "going to a restaurant" in the Seattle database. The operations dictionary (see Figure 4.2) is the skeleton of the Entity-Relationship Diagram. Each entry in the dictionary lists several entities that relate to one another. These relationships among entities in an operation's entries represent those relationships that in real life are needed to accomplish the operation. Thus *restaurant, telephone number,* and *directory* are related to one another through the operation *find telephone number.*

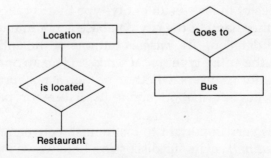

Figure 5.1. Graphic presentation of entities and relationships

The fact that they all appear in one entry in the operations dictionary indicates that when telephone numbers are recorded they should correspond to individual restaurants, and that a directory that includes telephone numbers should be available for the operation to be completed.

Operations, you may recall, are defined as the specific activities that together constitute a function. When one considers the Entity-Relationship Diagram for the function "Going to a restaurant," each operation represents a small portion of this diagram. One way to construct this diagram is, therefore, to integrate all the entities and relationships that are expressed in the operations dictionary.

Thus, to construct the diagram for a function, we create a mini-diagram for each operation in the operations dictionary. The operations *find telephone number* and *make reservations*, for example, would generate two mini-diagrams, as illustrated in Figure 5.2.

Theoretically, one could first go through the entire operations dictionary, draw a mini-diagram for each of the operations, and only then integrate the mini-diagrams. This approach is not practical, however. It is more efficient to integrate the mini-diagrams one by one in a gradual process as they are generated from the operations dictionary. Thus, we can first integrate the mini-diagram for *find telephone number* with the one for *make reservation* (Figure 5.3). Next we generate the mini-diagram for the following operation in the dictionary.

This example clearly illustrates the efficiency of this approach. The new and integrated mini-diagram (see Figure 5.3) is essentially the first mini-diagram (for *find telephone number*) with the addition of one relationship ("scheduled by") and one entity (*reservation schedule*).

As we represent additional operations, the integrated mini-diagram expands to include more relationships and entities. When we add operation P004, for example, to the integrated mini-diagram in Figure 5.3, we have a mini-diagram that includes the entity *type of food* (Figure 5.4).

For some operations, all the entities included in their entries are mentioned for the first time, and their mini-diagrams cannot be immediately integrated with those for the previous operations. Operation P006 presents an example of such a situation. Both en-

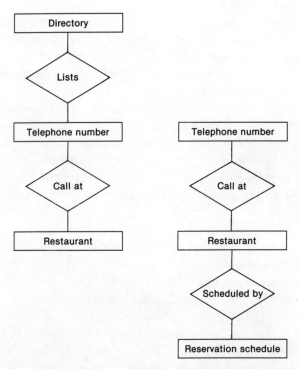

Figure 5.2. Mini-diagram for the operations **find telephone number** *and* **make reservation**

tities that are needed to accomplish this operation—*bus* and *bus schedule*—have not been listed before. Clearly, there is no straight-forward way in which the mini-diagram for this operation could be integrated with the diagram generated by all the previous operations.

The best way to resolve the problem is to start an additional mini-diagram separately from the integrated mini-diagram (Figure 5.5). Next, each of the following operations is considered for integration with both mini-diagrams. Our example exhibits an easy case because the next operation, *take bus* (P007), immediately forms the connection between the two mini-diagrams (Figure 5.6).

While such luck may not hold throughout the building of a graphic representation, as a designer analyzes additional operations, relationships between separated mini-diagrams will be es-

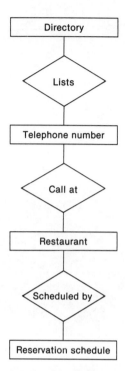

Figure 5.3. An integrated mini-diagram for both **find telephone number** *and* **make reservation**

tablished. If, however, when all the operations have been represented, some independent mini-diagrams still exist, checking each entity in the central mini-diagram may uncover relationships with entities in the isolated mini-diagrams. Once found, these relationships are established even though they were not expressed in the operations dictionary.

When all the operations from the operations dictionary are integrated into an Entity-Relationship Diagram, the major part of the diagram is completed. As a final check, we need to consider each item of data in the data dictionary to see whether it is represented in the diagram. In our example, the items *house specialties, price,* and *wait,* for instance, were not listed in the sample operations dictionary. In other words, they were not mentioned as items of data that are necessary for the accomplishment of an operation.

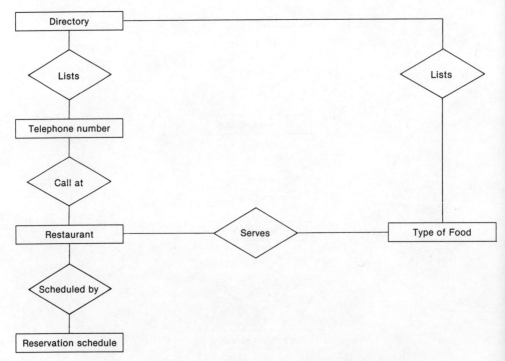

Figure 5.4. An integrated mini-diagram for three operations

There might be two reasons for this omission. First, these items of data, or some of them, might not be relevant to any operation that relates to the function "going to a restaurant." In this case, we should probably eliminate them from the data dictionary. Such an elimination, however, should not be taken lightly; before an elimination of any item of data, one must check and recheck to see if the item is indeed completely irrelevant to the function.

Second, the items might have been missed only because none of the sources, or the potential users, tied them with an operation they described. One must keep in mind that when users were selected, and information about potential use solicited, there was no guarantee of a comprehensive coverage of data requirements. Database designers can, therefore, complement the information derived from potential users. They should use their judgment to

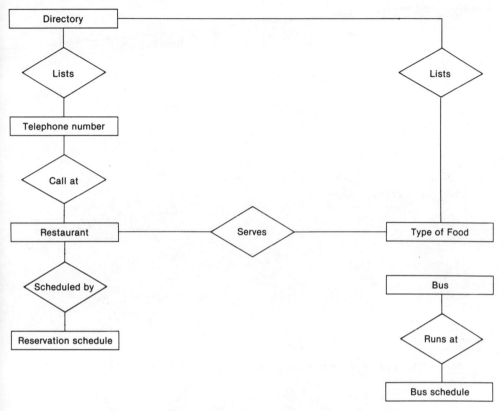

Figure 5.5. The mini-diagram for **consult bus schedule**

determine how these items of data should be related to other entities in the diagram and to establish the necessary relationships.

ATTRIBUTES

The last fundamental concept in the Entity-Relationship Model to
be defined is an attribute. An *attribute* is a piece of information
about an entity or about a relationship. *Cleanliness,* for example,
is an attribute of the entity *restaurant,* and so are the *name, price,*
or *address.* The entity *bus* may have *frequency* as its attribute, and

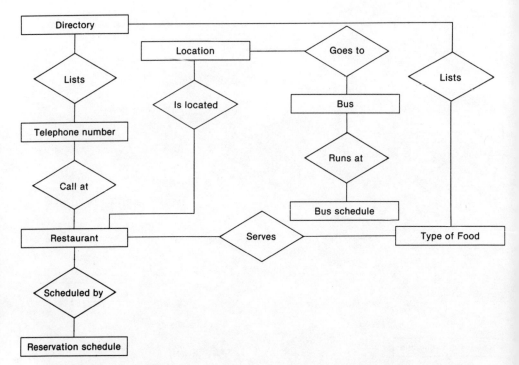

Figure 5.6. An integrated mini-diagram for the operations **consult bus schedule** *and* **take bus**

the *date* on which a restaurant had been reviewed by a reviewer is an attribute of the relationship "reviewed." Attributes are represented by circle-shaped boxes in the Entity-Relationship Diagram (Figure 5.7).

ENTITIES, RELATIONSHIPS, AND ATTRIBUTES

The construction of the Entity-Relationship Diagram requires constant checking and rechecking as additional mini-diagrams are integrated. This constant checking, in turn, requires an even more finely-tuned understanding of the three fundamental concepts just discussed. Here we look at various features of entities,

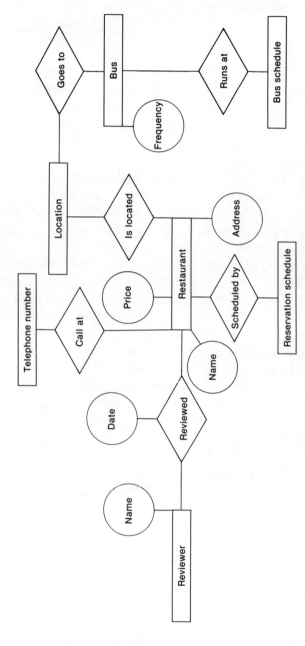

Figure 5.7. An example of entities, relationships, and attributes

relationships, and attributes, and highlight aspects that require special attention.

Focal Entities

An Entity-Relationship Diagram may have some entities in it that are more "central" than others. In most of the figures in this chapter, and particularly in Figure 5.6 and 5.7, the entity *restaurant* has more relationships and more attributes than any other. This is not surprising, given that we are building the diagram for the function "Going to a restaurant." It stands to reason, then, that most entities and attributes relate in one way or another to the entity *restaurant*. An entity that is central to an Entity-Relationship Diagram is called a *focal entity*. A single diagram may have more than one focal entity.

While not all diagrams have focal entities, the concept remains important. Pointing to focal entities facilitates an additional validity check: Each entity in the diagram can be checked to determine whether or not it can be related to a focal entity. The relationships between each entity and the focal entity are not necessarily direct: An entity may relate to a focal entity through other entities. The entity *bus*, for example, does not relate directly to *restaurant*; but once it is known where a restaurant is located, one can find the bus that runs to the restaurant.

An Instance of an Entity

Once the relationships among entities are established, designers proceed to check the usefulness of the descriptions of items of data in the data dictionary. One can perform such checks on two levels.

First, it is necessary to examine whether all the elements that are mentioned in the description of an entity are explicitly related to the entity in the diagram. We can check, for example, if all the elements in the description of *restaurant* are indeed represented in the sample diagram. The description of a restaurant in our data dictionary is, "A place where people who do not reside in it are served meals for a fee." The first element in this description ("a place where . . . ") indicates that a restaurant is located somewhere, a fact that is described in the diagram as illustrated in Figure 5.7. In addition, meals are served in a restaurant. While this element is not represented directly in the diagram, it is mentioned implicitly in the relationship "serves" and the entity *type of food*. The last element in this example is the fee that is charged in a restaurant. Here again the element is represented indirectly because the price that is charged in a restaurant is an attribute of the entity *restaurant* (see Figure 5.7).

Ordinarily, a designer should check for contradictions or disagreements between the descriptions in the data dictionary and the diagram, as well as for additional elements that should be represented. These examinations may result in modifications in the descriptions, and they may lead to the creation of new entities, which are then recorded in both the Entity-Relationship Diagram and the data dictionary.

Second, it is advisable to run through a hypothetical sample of individual entities, and check if the definitions, relationships, and attributes make sense. For the entity *restaurant*, we may want to consider some familiar restaurants and test if the attributes and the relationships established for that entity can be easily derived.

Consider, for example, the restaurant PauPau. According to the Yellow Pages, it serves Cantonese food in Chinatown but classic Chinese and Chinese–American in its downtown branch. The two restaurants have the same name and the same owner. Are they one restaurant with two branches or are they two different restaurants?

At this point we have nothing to guide us in our decision. Why not consider the PauPau branches as two different restaurants? After all, they are located in different places and serve different types of food. These two "restaurants," however, have the same name. Therefore, we need to make a note to ourselves that the name of a restaurant is not necessarily unique.

Alternatively, we can consider PauPau as one restaurant that has two locations, each with a different type of food. To designate which type of food is served in each location, we need to establish a relationship that links the entities *location* with *type of food*. In other words, if we choose the later option, we need to establish a new relationship.

The notion of establishing a new relationship should not be

alarming here because PauPau is not the only restaurant with branches in various neighborhoods in the city. Thus, if we add a relationship between *location* and *type of food*, we can assume it would hold true for many restaurants. The problem is, however, that different branches of a restaurant usually serve the same type of food. The new relationship we would have to establish therefore, is not very useful. For the PauPau restaurant, the first option—to list its branches as two distinct restaurants—is the sounder solution.

Consider, however, an extreme—but utterly realistic—example: the McBurger chain of restaurants. It has about 50 branches in town, and each branch serves exactly the same food, charges the same prices, and even looks very much like the others. Shall we follow here the example set by the PauPau restaurant and enter data about 50 distinct restaurants?

Clearly, the option that is suitable for the first example does not apply here. In a sense, we can say that McBurger is one restaurant but with many locations. While a reviewer may need to write one review for the downtown PauPau and another for its Chinatown branch, it is certainly not necessary to write a review about each and every McBurger place in town.

What is the difference between PauPau and McBurger? The branches of PauPau are *essentially different* from one another and need, therefore, to be considered as distinct restaurants. The branches of McBurger are *essentially the same*, and their number and locations may change frequently; it is more efficient, therefore, to consider them as one restaurant.

However convincing this argument, it is not rigorous enough for database design. We must state explicitly the meanings of the comparisons *essentially different* and *essentially the same*. In other words, given the entities, relationships, and attributes, we have to decide which features are *essential* to a restaurant, and which are not so essential or may require frequent updating. Because the *name, type of food,* and the *price* range are typical of a chain of restaurants and are not likely to go through frequent changes, we can decide that if the branches of a restaurant have the same name, serve the same type of food, and charge the same price range, they all are to be considered as one restaurant. And if one of the conditions is not fulfilled, each branch must then be considered as a distinct restaurant.

We could write this rule as an addition to the diagram and ask data collectors to refer to it when they need to decide whether an establishment is one or more restaurants. For ease of data collection, however, it is better to incorporate this decision into the diagram so that it becomes part of the general schema, rather than an addendum.

Here we can first modify the description of *restaurant* to "a place that has a certain name, serves a certain type of food, and charges a certain fee." This new entity is different from the previous one. It does not represent a set of actual restaurants, but rather a set of "concepts of restaurants." McBurger, which is one restaurant, is actually the "McBurger concept." It is determined, in other words, by the type of food and the price that is charged. So is TacoTell or Atlantic Desserts, which has three branches in town, because they too serve the same food and charge the same price in all their branches.

The restaurants themselves are then represented in the entity *instance of restaurant.* Thus we can say that the McBurger place around the corner is an instance of the McBurger concept, or an instance of the McBurger restaurant. Instances of a restaurant have their own locations, their own telephone numbers, and their own addresses (Figure 5.8).

Separating an entity from an instance of an entity is a reliable mechanism for avoiding repetition of identical pieces of data, but it can serve other purposes as well. To demonstrate its advantages, let us consider the movie section of the Seattle database. A movie is an artistic creation regardless of whether or not it is screened at a certain point in time. Screen writers, producers, actors, and directors were involved in its creation; it was produced in a certain place; it receives a certain rating; and it belongs to a certain genre. All that is involved in the creation of a movie is related to the entity *movie.*

Each copy of a movie, mounted on reels, is an *instance of movie.* A copy is shown at a certain movie theater, it may or may not have subtitles, it may be edited (as for special television screenings), and it is shown at a certain time.

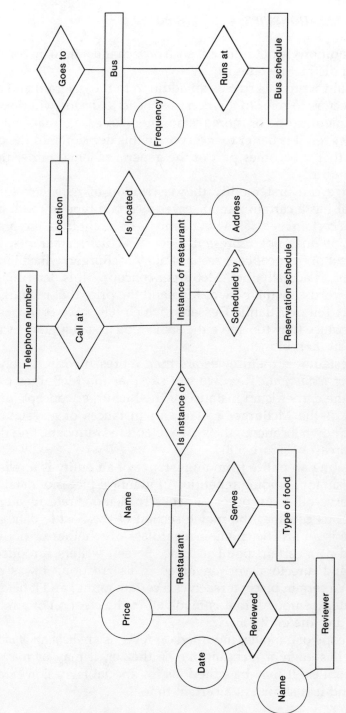

Figure 5.8. A representation of the entities restaurant *and* instance of restaurant

Because a movie can be shown in a number of theaters around town, it is efficient to have all the information about a movie with one entity, and the information about a particular copy in another. This arrangement facilitates, in addition, a new class of requests: those for general information about movies. All the information about a movie is related to one entity—*movie*—and is located in one place. It is readily available whether or not the movie is showing in any theater.

Thus in defining the two concepts *entity* and *instance of entity*, a designer separates features that are essential or characteristic of entities from features that, while important to a database, are not typical or may require constant updating. Note, however, that while the distinction between these concepts is important on the conceptual level, in practice the term *instance* is not self-explanatory and may sometimes be confusing. To represent these two concepts, one might prefer to use terms that are more familiar, such as *chain of restaurants* and *restaurant*, or *movie* and *copy of movie*.

Establishing Relationships

Each mini-diagram represents entities and relationships that are needed to accomplish an operation that is recorded in the operations dictionary. Each entry in the operations dictionary, however, provides us with a list of entities that are related to one another but there is no guidance as to how the entities should be related. Our first example involved the entities *bus*, *location*, and *restaurant*. In Figure 5.1 we established one relationship between *restaurant* and *location* and another between *location* and *bus*.

A legitimate question here is, Why not establish one relationship between *restaurant* and *location*, and another between *restaurant* and *bus*, as illustrated in Figure 5.9? This arrangement makes sense because users are not interested in buses in general but rather in buses that go to restaurants. With this kind of relationship arrangement, each restaurant is directly related to the buses that people can take when they need to get to the restaurant.

Here again we want to compare the efficiency of the two options. True, a direct relationship between *restaurant* and *bus* facil-

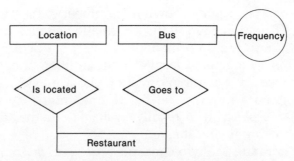

Figure 5.9. An alternate graphic presentation of the relationships among the entities restaurant, location, *and* bus

itates fast retrieval of bus numbers for a given restaurant, but it may lead to unnecessary repetition when a number of restaurants can be reached by the same buses because they are located in the same vicinity. Consider a food circle, or an eatery, where over 30 restaurants are located in one building, each providing its own specialties. Another example is a large shopping mall that houses a number of restaurants. If we had a direct relationship between *restaurant* and *bus,* data collectors would have to list the same bus numbers—those that go to the shopping mall—each time they enter information about a restaurant in the mall. In addition, every time they enter a bus number they would have to repeatedly record its frequency. This routine is clearly inefficient.

Another issue that we may want to consider when we have doubts about how to relate entities is whether or not these entities (such as *bus*) are likely to appear in Entity-Relationship diagrams for *other* functions. The movie section of our database, for instance, would probably include the entities *location* and *bus* also, as would other sections such as the museum or concert sections. When we integrate all the sections of a database into one schema, and if we keep the direct relationship between entities such as *restaurant, movie theater, museum,* or *concert hall,* and the entity *bus,* bus numbers that go to one location would be repeated whenever the location houses more than one kind of establishment. We may conclude, therefore, that although we gather information about establishments rather than about locations, buses go to certain locations that house the establishments about which we collect information.

Another issue that requires a decision when relationships are established is what name to give a relationship. Should we, for instance, use the name "goes to" for the relationships between *bus* and *location*—as in, a bus goes to a location? Or, should we prefer "can be reached by"—as in, a location can be reached by a bus?

Intuitively, a shorter name is better. This decision is supported by the previous discussion about the names of items of data. Here too, one gives a name to a relationship so it can be identified distinctly and recognized among other relationships in a database, but the name does not reflect any *properties* of the relationship to which it is assigned. Relationships are established between two entities (or more, as we see next) and they have no predetermined direction; if a *restaurant*, for example, "serves" a specific *type of food*, that specific *type of food* "is served" in the *restaurant*. The properties of relationships are explicitly recorded in the data dictionary as explained in Chapter 7, "Data Dictionary Entries for Relationships."

The name of a relationship must be unique, but we should also attempt to apply terms that reflect the nature of the relationship. Later on, when relationships are recorded in the data dictionary, we will add a code that identifies the "direction" of each relationship.

Multiple-Entity Relationships

The relationships established in the previous examples were limited to sets of two entities. At times, however, a relationship lies among more than two entities. Consider, for instance, the portion of the Entity-Relationship Diagram for the function "Going to a restaurant" that represents the restaurant review process. The three entities that are involved in this portion are *restaurant, reviewer,* and the *grade* that is given by a reviewer. At first, one might be tempted to establish two distinct relationships: one between *restaurant* and *reviewer,* and another between *reviewer* and *grade* (Figure 5.10).

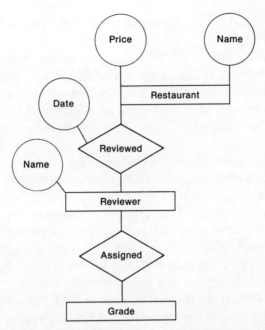

Figure 5.10. A representation of the entities restaurant, reviewer, *and* grade

This arrangement facilitates the retrieval of a list of reviewers who reviewed a certain restaurant and for each reviewer, a list of grades that he has assigned. Looking at these lists, however, a user would not be able to tell which grades have been assigned to a certain restaurant because a *grade* is not related to a *restaurant*.

An alternative then is to relate *grade* directly to *restaurant*, as shown is Figure 5.11. Here, however, we would not be able to answer a question such as, What grade did Mr. Smith assign to the Minaret restaurant? Keeping in mind that people may be interested in grades that have been assigned by a certain reviewer, we would like to have a database that could answer such a question.

In other words, we need to establish a three-way relationship that binds together *restaurant*, *reviewer*, and *grade*. The graphic presentation of this relationship—"reviewed and graded"—is sketched in Figure 5.12. Here, for each restaurant we can list the

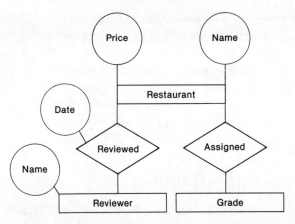

Figure 5.11. An alternate representation of the entities, **restaurant, reviewer,** *and* **grade**

reviewers who have reviewed it, and for each, the grade that he has assigned to the restaurant.

After establishing this relationship, we may speculate that some users may want to know the average grade given by a certain reviewer. To answer this question a user needs the list of all

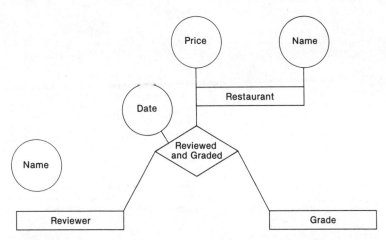

Figure 5.12. A representation of the relationship "reviewed and graded"

the grades given by that reviewer. With the new relationship, she would need to get the list of grades assigned by the reviewer to each restaurant. To retrieve this information she would have to enter, one by one, the names of all the restaurants that have been reviewed by that person. This is obviously an undesirable situation. To cover as many different uses of a database as possible, we can establish an additional relationship, "assigned," between the entities *reviewer* and *grade* (Figure 5.13).

Entities versus Attributes

The restaurant review process in the Entity-Relationship Diagram for the function "Going to a restaurant" can be presented through yet another configuration, as illustrated in Figure 5.14. The entities *restaurant* and *reviewer* are connected by two distinct relationships: "reviewed" and "graded." In addition, *grade* is no longer an entity but rather an attribute of the relationship graded. This configuration can facilitate response to questions such as, Which grades were assigned to a restaurant by a certain reviewer; which grades were assigned to a restaurant by all its reviewers;

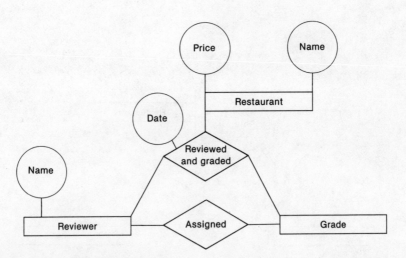

Figure 5.13. A representation of the relationships that associate the entities **restaurant, reviewer,** *and* **grade**

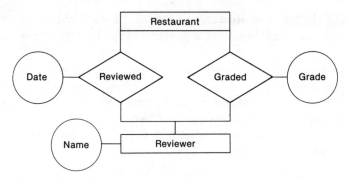

Figure 5.14. A representation of the relationships between the entities **restaurant** *and* **reviewer,** *with* **grade** *as an attribute*

and which grades have been assigned by a certain reviewer to all restaurants?

This new configuration raises two issues. First, it represents the fact that two entities can be connected by more than one relationship. In our example, a reviewer performs two distinct operations with regard to restaurants: review and grading. Hence the entities *restaurant* and *reviewer* are connected by two distinct relationships.

Second, *grade*, which was an entity in the previous configuration, is here an attribute. This change brings to mind the question, How can one tell whether an item of data should be represented as an entity or as an attribute?

Entities are distinguishable objects, and attributes are pieces of information about entities or relationships. The distinction between the two is not always easy to determine. It is easy to see, for instance, that *bus* is an entity rather than an attribute, even though we are only interested in a bus if it goes to a restaurant. We can also make a relatively clear case that *reviewer* is an entity because a reviewer is not just a piece of information about a restaurant, but a person that has individual qualities.

It is more difficult to decide, however, whether *grade* is a distinct entity or whether it is a piece of information about the process of grading a restaurant. In fact, there is no objective method of determining the identity of *grade* or of similar objects. Here again, the decision about how to represent such objects must rely on design specifications. As a general rule, we can state:

> An object or a fact is an attribute when it is not of interest by itself but only when it is connected to one, and only one, entity or relationship, and, in addition, it has no attributes itself. If, however, an object or a fact might be of interest regardless of the entities and relationships to which it is connected, or if it has attributes, it must be classified as an entity.

This general rule can guide a decision about the status of *grade*. Suppose restaurants in a city have a number of directories, each including information about restaurants with assigned grades that were "approved" by the directory's editorial board. Let us assume also that each such directory has a distinct character. Thus, if you are really picky about food, you should probably consult the "Eat in Style" directory because it includes only those grades that have been assigned after a meticulous review. But if you just like to eat well, you might want to consult the "Hearty Eater" which includes grades extracted from reviews written by people with no credentials but their love for food.

In other words, the grades themselves, independent of the restaurants to which they were assigned or of the reviewers who assigned them, are of interest: They have characteristics that determine in which directory they should be cited. In this case, we probably should indicate for each grade the directories in which it is cited. Here we need to select *grade* as an entity and make a connection with the entity *directory*. If, however, grades are of interest only in relation to the restaurant to which they have been assigned or to the reviewer who assigned them, we could select *grade* as an attribute.

Following the same rule and rationale, we probably want to reverse our decision about *telephone number*. At this point it seems that these numbers are of interest only when they are used to call a particular restaurant, or any other establishment. As illustrated in Figure 5.15, *telephone number* is an attribute.

Another example is the entity *type of food*. While it is reasonable to assume that type of food is of interest only when it is served in a certain restaurant, and thus the entity should be an attribute,

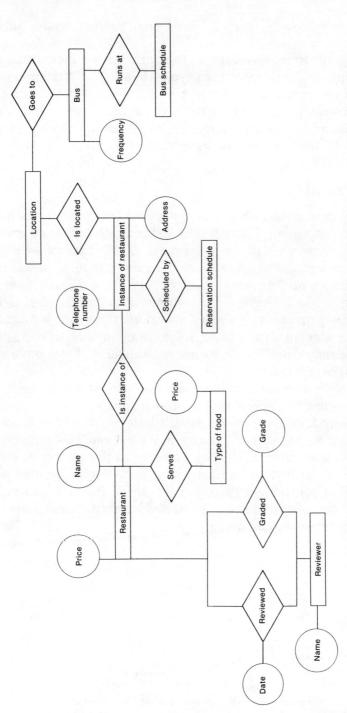

Figure 5.15. A representation of a portion of the Entity-Relationship Diagram for the function "Going to a restaurant"

115

we may want to leave things as they are. As we mentioned before, people might be interested in a certain type of food independently of the restaurants in which it is served. A requester may want to know, for example, what is the average price of Chinese food. If we anticipate such a request, we need to keep *type of food* as an entity and add *price* as its attribute (see Figure 5.15).

Divided Attributes

An entity or a relationship may have an attribute that has more than one component. Consider, for example, the attribute *price* of the entity *restaurant*. While restaurants usually charge a distinct range of prices, some have more than one range. A restaurant may offer a menu for regular dinners, and also a menu for people who would like to have a light dinner after the theater. Other restaurants provide inexpensive selections for lunch but charge dearly for elegant dinners. As we examine a sample of restaurants, we may conclude that quite a number of them have two price ranges: high and low.

If this split in price is indeed common among restaurants, we certainly want to represent it in the database. For our Entity-Relationship Model we divide the attribute *price* into two kinds of prices: high and low. In the diagram, we indicate this division by using two lines from the entity pointing to the attribute. While the name of the attribute is unchanged, each line is qualified with the relevant component (Figure 5.16). In an Entity-Relationship Diagram, some attributes would be divided into components and some would not be divided at all.

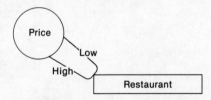

Figure 5.16. An example of a divided attribute

SUMMARY

The Entity-Relationship Model is used to represent items of data and the relationships among them that are specific to a database. It is based on the concepts of entities, relationships, and attributes. The Entity-Relationship Diagram is a graphic presentation of entities and their attributes and relationships.

An *entity* is a "thing" that can be distinctly identified. An individual restaurant, a particular telephone number, and a specific bus number are examples of entities in a city database. In the construction of the conceptual schema of a database, however, we are interested in sets of entities of the same types, such as *restaurants, telephone numbers,* or *buses,* rather than in individual entities. Each such set is called an *entity type.*

A database designer must draw a clear distinction between *entities* and *entity types.* While for most items of data this distinction is quite straightforward, some items may require a close examination of the level of detail that is desirable before a decision about what constitutes an entity type can be made. For the sake of simplicity, *entity types* are called *entities* in this book.

A *relationship* is an association among entities. The entities *restaurant* and *type of food,* for example, are associated by the relationship "serves." An *attribute* is a piece of information about an entity or about a relationship. For instance, the *address* of a restaurant is an attribute of the entity *restaurant,* and the *date* on which a restaurant has been reviewed by a reviewer is an attribute of the relationship "reviewed."

The Entity-Relationship Diagram is constructed according to the entries in the operations dictionary. Each entry represents one or more relationships that exist among the items of data involved. Each such entry generates a mini-diagram to represent the entities and their relationships and attributes that are important for the completion of an operation. The mini-diagrams are gradually integrated to form the Entity-Relationship Diagram for the function for which the operations dictionary was constructed.

A diagram may have one or more entities that are more central than others. These entities are called *focal entities.* Recognizing their role provides a useful validity check, because each entity in the diagram needs to be associated, directly or indirectly, with at least one focal entity.

Further examination of the nature of entities reveals that items of data that have several instances generate two concepts: an *entity* and an *instance of entity*. The *entity* concept represents the relationships and attributes that are essential to the item of data, such as the director, actors, or producers of a movie. Attributes and relationships that are not typical, or that require constant updating, are represented by the *instance of entity* concept, such as the movie theater or the time at which a movie is shown.

At times a database designer will have difficulty deciding whether a certain item of data is an entity or an attribute. Such a distinction is determined by design specifications and is guided by the rule, if an item of data is not of interest by itself but only when it is connected to one—and only one—entity or relationship, and if, in addition, it has no attributes, it is an attribute.

As the Entity-Relationship Diagram for a function is constructed, a designer may see that one relationship associates more than two entities; the relationship "reviewed and graded," for instance, can be established to connect the entity *restaurant* with the entities *reviewer* and *grade*. Along the same line, two entities can be associated with one another through more than one relationship. The entities *restaurant* and *reviewer*, for example, can be connected by two relationships, "reviewed" and "graded." In addition, an attribute may have more than one component. For example, to represent pricing practice of restaurants, the attribute *price* of food may need to be divided into two "types" of price: high and low.

Now that we understand the basic nature of Entity-Relationship diagrams and their components—entities, relationships, and attributes—we can examine the construction of the global diagram for a database, as well as the rules that define and explain the conceptual schema.

REFERENCE

1. Chen, P. P.-S. 1976. "The Entity-Relationship Model—Towards a Unified View of Data." *ACM Transactions on Database Systems*, Vol. 1, no. 1, pp. 9–36.

6

THE INTEGRATION OF SCHEMATA

Using the Entity-Relationship Model, each function is represented by its Entity-Relationship Diagram and the data dictionary of the function. To establish the conceptual schema of a database, these schemata are gradually integrated. Schemata for one subject area within one environment are first integrated, one after the other, to create a temporary global schema. Schemata for functions in the same subject area but within the next environment are then integrated into the ever-growing temporary global schema. Next, schemata for other subject areas are gradually added, thus creating the global schema, which represents all functions across all subject areas and environments. Schemata are integrated by resolving conflicts between names and definitions as well as conflicts in inclusion, and by modifying and integrating local data dictionaries.

Now that the nature of the Entity-Relationship Model is clear, it is time to examine again from the beginning the process of database design. To analyze the requirements of potential users, designers first divide the enterprise into environments, with each one representing a distinct group of potential uses for a database.

For each environment they then identify the subject areas involved, such as restaurants, movies, and social services. To collect requirements within each environment, they further divide each subject area into functions, such as "Going to a restaurant," "Dining in a restaurant," and "Reviewing a restaurant"; and for each of the functions, they create data and operations dictionaries.

Each operations dictionary guides the construction of the Entity-Relationship Diagram for the pertinent function. In our example, we constructed part of the diagram for the function "Going to a restaurant." The Entity-Relationship Diagram, the pertinent entries in the data dictionary, and the relevant set of rules together create the conceptual schema for a function.

To build the conceptual schema for the whole database, a designer must integrate the diagrams for the individual functions. During this process they also modify the entries in the data dictionary, as needed, and establish the rules for each entity, relationship, and attribute. In other words, to build the global schema that represents all the data to be included in a database, we integrate the local Entity-Relationship Diagrams—those constructed for each function—into one diagram, update the data dictionary, and establish rules for data collection. This chapter discusses the first two processes. The nature of the rules to be formulated is described in Chapter 7.

While the three processes—creating the global diagram, updating the data dictionary, and establishing rules—are described here in a linear fashion (one process following the other), in actual database design they are performed simultaneously. The integration of, say, two diagrams almost always requires an update of the data dictionary and the formulation of new rules at the same time. Later steps in the integration may require the modification of newly established revisions in the data dictionary or of rules just created. Building a global schema is an iterative process in which many processes and steps affect previous decisions; it requires constant modifications.

The construction of the global schema follows a procedure similar to the one used for the construction of a local, or function-bound, schema. To construct a local schema designers gradually integrate mini-diagrams that are generated from individual operations and update the data dictionary accordingly. They gradually integrate local schemata, established for functions, to construct the global schema.

The division into environments, subject areas, and functions is a useful guide in the process of schemata integration. Designers first integrate all the schemata for functions in the same subject area and within one environment. Thus we first integrate the schemata for the functions "Going to a restaurant" and "Dining in a restaurant." Now we have a schema—and in particular, an Entity-Relationship Diagram—that describes two functions within the subject area "restaurants" within the clientele environment. This is the first temporary global schema. We then integrate another schema within the same subject—say, "Reviewing a restaurant"—with the first temporary global schema to create the second temporary global schema. We continue to enlarge our temporary global schema by integrating additional functions from the restaurants subject area within the clientele environment to construct the temporary global schema that describes all the functions within this subject area.

Next we examine the other environments and check if they have a similar subject area. If the administration environment has restaurants as a subject area, we integrate its local schemata, one after the other, into the ever-growing temporary global schema. When all the functions are integrated, the temporary global schema describes the subject area restaurants within two environments: the clientele and the administration.

Once the temporary global schema describes all the functions related to a subject area and within all relevant environments, it is time to consider the next subject area. Here we start integrating local schemata from, say, the movies section with the temporary global schema for the restaurants section. We continue with this process until all the schemata for the functions in this subject area are integrated with the temporary global schema, and then move to the next subject area.

The schema that is created after all the local schemata have been integrated is the global schema for that database—that is, the schema that represents all the data to be included in the database.

One should note that while the process of integration described here addresses schemata constructed for a database design, it can be used for *database integration* as well. In practice, organizations are frequently interested in integrating several existing databases. Integrating the conceptual schemata of such databases in the gradual process described here is a useful method for database integration. Those who have been involved in such projects can appreciate how the systematic nature of the process improves reliability and saves much time and effort.

The applicability of this method to database integration also emphasizes the vital role of a methodical construction of the conceptual schema for a database. Clearly, many problems associated with the integration of databases that do not have conceptual schema, or those that were constructed using a trial–and–error method, could have been alleviated if the databases had been constructed with a systematic and well-documented approach.

How to integrate schemata? What is the procedure to create one schema that represents more than one function? The process of integrating schemata is a process of *conflict resolution*: each entity, relationship, and attribute in one schema is checked to determine its place in the other schema. For example, the entity *restaurant* appears both in the "Going to a restaurant" and in the "Dining in a restaurant" schema. We need to ascertain that these two occurrences of the entity are indeed identical—in other words, they have the same description in the data dictionary; they have the same attributes; and attributes in one schema are not entities in the other. Once we iron out any conflicts, we can integrate these two occurrences into one occurrence of the entity *restaurant*.

In resolution of conflict we are guided by the Entity-Relationship Diagram. We also constantly consult the data dictionary. Final decisions about modifications in the data dictionary, however, are frequently postponed until the Entity-Relationship Diagram for the global schema is completed.

CONFLICT RESOLUTION

As we can see from the previous example, certain kinds of conflicts tend to occur. We can list these kinds of conflicts, and the modifications of the Entity-Relationship Diagram for the temporary global schema that their resolution requires. The following discussion describes three kinds of conflicts: those arising between names, definitions, and in inclusion. Its structure is partially based on a paper by Peter Pin-Shan Chen [1].

Conflicts between Names

Name conflicts occur when the names selected for entities, relationships, or attributes are inconsistent between two schemata. When two schemata are integrated, entities that have the same name may or may not be identical; conversely, entities that have different names might be identical. This type of conflict may also occur between relationships and attributes in two schemata.

When checking for name conflicts, a designer must be particularly cautious and examine whether entities that are seemingly different (or identical) refer to different (or identical) objects, regardless of their names. Consider again the entity *restaurant*, which appears in two schemata: "Going to a restaurant" and "Dining in a restaurant." The description of *restaurant* in one schema may be different from the description in the other. It is likely, however, that the two versions represent the same object: Both descriptions refer to what we know to be restaurants. Here we do not really have a conflict because one name is used for the same object. To resolve the inconsistency in entity description, we must update the data dictionary, a process described later.

In some instances, however, the same name may be used to represent objects that are indeed different. The term *bus* is a good example. It is used in the schema for the function "Going to a restaurant" to designate a fleet of buses running a particular route. For this function we are not interested in individual vehicles, but rather in those that run along a certain route. Now suppose the bus company belongs to the city. At least one schema for the administration environment is likely to include the entity *bus*. City administration, however, is interested in individual vehicles: they need to assign drivers to vehicles; they need to record the location of each vehicle; and they have a maintenance schedule for each bus.

The object that is presented by the entity *bus* in the clientele environment is different from the object that is presented by the same entity in the administration environment. It is necessary, therefore, to make a clear distinction between these two entities that happen to share the same name.

In contrast, two (or more) entities or attributes that are identical—or that can be considered identical for the purpose of the database—may have different names. The Entity-Relationship Diagram for the function "Going to a restaurant" provides an example. There *cleanliness* is an attribute of the entity *restaurant*. At the same time, the diagram for the function "Licensing a restaurant," which is in the administration environment, may include the attribute *health hazards*. These two attributes are probably very similar, if not identical, to one another. We can, therefore, go back and find out what standards the city uses to determine whether or not a restaurant is a health hazard. We may find that city inspectors indeed determine this fact by the degree of the restaurant's cleanliness.

If we find that these two attributes are actually identical, we can represent them in the integrated schema as one attribute, and choose one of the attribute names as a temporary solution. Later, when we update the data dictionary, we can make a more informed decision about a preferred name, because there might be other named entities or attributes that point out the cleanliness of a restaurant.

Conflicts between Definitions

Definition conflicts occur when an entity in one schema overlaps an entity in another, but the definitions of the two are not completely identical. Such conflicts may also occur between relationships or between attributes. The common method to resolve these kinds of conflicts is to split or to merge entity types, relationships, or attributes. The decision to split or to merge is based on design specifications and on individual circumstances.

Splitting Entity Types. In some cases the best method to resolve a definition conflict between two entity types is to split the entity type with the broader definition into a number of entities, each defined more narrowly that the original one.

Consider a situation where potential users in the city administration, who were consulted for the database design, lead a designer to conclude that all city officials who are involved with restaurants should be included in one entity. The designer then represents all people who are responsible for inspecting, protecting, or licensing a restaurant in one entity—*person*. This portion of the Entity-Relationship Diagram is presented in Figure 6.1: Each restaurant is related to the people in the city administration who are involved with its operation.

In the clientele schema, you may recall, restaurants are related to people in a more specific manner; each restaurant is related to the reviewers who reviewed and graded it, as illustrated in Figure 5.15. (For simplicity's sake, let us assume that there is only one relationship between *restaurant* and *reviewer*: "reviewed.") This discrepancy should probe a designer to find out if users in the clientele environment would like to see people in city administration also related to restaurants in a specific manner. Suppose the designer discovers that restaurant owners require each type of city official to be represented in a distinct manner, and clearly separated from reviewers. To achieve an integrated schema that is useful to all users, he can split the entity type *person* in the administration schema into its detailed components. Each group of people is then represented explicitly as a separate entity (Figure 6.2). This representation enables users to get information about people who are involved with restaurants according to their task.

Merging Entity Types. The opposite approach to the resolution of definition conflicts between entities is to merge the entities that

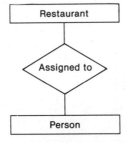

Figure 6.1. The relationship between **restaurant** *and* **person** *in the administration schema*

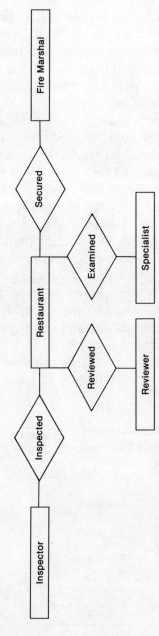

Figure 6.2. Representation of the relationship between restaurant and people who are involved in the integrated schema after splitting the entity person

overlap and thus create a new entity with a definition that is broader than the definitions of the merged entities.

Consider the previous problem. To achieve the same end, a designer could have selected an alternate resolution: merge the entity *reviewer* in the clientele schema with the entity *person* in the administration schema (Figure 6.3). Here we create a new entity that includes *all* people who are involved with restaurants; the entity *person* is no longer limited to city officials. Reviewers, however, are distinguished from city personnel by the unique relationship "reviewed" that exists between them and restaurants, as are inspectors or fire marshals. This is a hint for what is yet to come: A merger of entities may require a change in the relationships associated with these entities, such as a split or a merger.

The choice between splitting or merging entity types is determined by specific design requirements. A reason for the choice of the latter might be a need for a central list of all people who are associated with restaurants—say, for tax purposes, or because quite a few perform more than one function. While all persons are represented in one entity, their functional relationships with restaurants can be determined by the set of relationships established to associate *person* with *restaurant*.

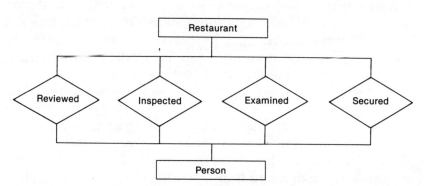

Figure 6.3. Representation of the relationship between **restaurant** *and* **person** *in the integrated schema after merging entity types*

Splitting Relationships. A definition conflict between relationships exists when a relationship in one schema overlaps a relationship in another, but the definitions of the two relationships are not completely identical. In some cases of this kind of conflict, it is best to split a broad relationship into a number of more specific relationships.

The last example of entity merger (see Figure 6.3) is also an example of a relationship split. The relationship "assigned to" (see Figure 6.1) is split into its components: "inspected," "examined," and "secured."

This example illustrates how a conflict can be resolved in more than one way. By representing city employees by their function, a designer can either split an entity type into its explicit components (e.g., *person* into *inspector, specialist,* and *fire marshal*), or merge entities (*person* with *reviewer*) and at the same time split a relationship. It should be noted here that relationships can be split without a merger of entities. For instance, the relationship "assigned to" could have been decomposed into its components without merging the entity *reviewer* with the entity *person* as originally perceived. Using this representation, a user can retrieve information about specific tasks that are performed for each restaurant.

Merging Relationships. The opposite approach to the resolution of definition conflicts between relationships is to merge the relationships that overlap into one relationship with a definition that is broader than each of its components. This approach is not likely to be used for schemata integration but may be useful to accommodate changes occurring in the enterprise—or in the environment—of a database during its lifetime.

To illustrate a merger of relationships, consider the relationships between the entities *bus route* and *time* (not shown in previous figures). Suppose a database designer concludes that complete schedule information should be given to each user inquiring about a certain bus. Suppose also that bus schedules during weekdays are different from those for weekends. To provide accurate and reliable information, the designer may decide to associate *bus route* with *time* through two relationships: "runs on weekdays" and "runs on weekends" (Figure 6.4).

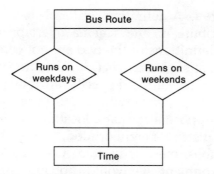

Figure 6.4. Representation of the relationship between **bus route** *and* **time** *when two schedules are maintained*

Suppose now that after the database has been in operation for a few years, the bus company decides to introduce a uniform schedule for buses—no more special schedule for weekends. The two relationships should then be merged into one, "runs" (Figure 6.5). This merger is necessary for at least two reasons. First, since weekday and weekend schedules are one and the same for each bus, schedule information can be recorded in one place only. Second, the relationships established for a database should reflect actual association; if there is only one type of schedule, no distinction between types of schedule should be represented in the database. A split may be confusing to database operators and users and introduce errors.

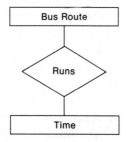

Figure 6.5. Representation of the relationship between **bus route** *and* **time** *when one schedule is maintained*

Splitting Attributes. A definition conflict between attributes exists when an attribute in one schema overlaps an attribute in another, but the definitions of the two are not completely identical. In some cases of such a conflict, it is best to split the broader attribute into a number of more specific attributes.

Consider the entity *location* with its attribute *name* (not shown in Figure 5.15). Suppose also that a location of an establishment is defined as the district, neighborhood, or the shopping center in which the establishment is located. Creating the schema for the clientele environment, we would probably consider the *name* of a location to be any name commonly used by the public. Using such an open and flexible definition for the name of a location may result in some locations having more than one name. City personnel, however, would probably require that each location have a unique name, and therefore, they are likely to assign a name to a location by the official name of its district or its neighborhood.

Once we integrate the clientele schema with those of the administration environment, therefore, a closer look is needed at the descriptions of each attribute. The public, we may discover, is not always familiar with the official names of shopping centers. Clearly, in this case the *name* of a location is often one thing to the public and another to the administration. In other words, a location has two "types" of names: the one that is known and used by the public, and the one for official matters. In the integrated schema, we have two attributes: the *official name* and the *common name*, both attached to one integrated entity—*location*.

Another consideration that supports this decision, and which is discussed later, lies in the need to identify each location uniquely. While one location may have more than one common name, it is most likely to have only one official name, and this name is probably not assigned to any other location. We can, therefore, use the official name to identify each location uniquely. On the other hand, we want to represent the common names of locations in the database because these are likely to be used by tourists and residents. A clear distinction is necessary between the two types of name—a distinction that can be achieved most easily by separating official names from the common ones.

Similar conflicts can be resolved with less radical steps: An attribute can be divided, rather than be split. To illustrate, let us consider the *telephone number* of a restaurant. The entry for this attribute in the data dictionary for the clientele environment specifies that one should call this number for reservations and information. City personnel, on the other hand, call restaurants to talk to their managers. The telephone number in which they are interested, therefore, is the management number. Here again we have two types of an attribute. This case, however, does not necessarily require the establishment of two distinct attributes. One type of telephone number is similar in nature to the other, and they are equally important to the database. In fact, for some restaurants the reservation and the management numbers are one and the same. In an integrated schema, therefore, we can divide the attribute *telephone number* into two types: *reservation* and *management* (Figure 6.6).

The decision whether to split an attribute or whether to just divide it depends on its domain—a concept that is introduced in Chapter 7. The rule of thumb is: If a conflict resolution requires that the domain be split, then the attribute must be split as well; if, however, the resolution of a conflict does not affect the domain or requires only some modifications, the attribute could be divided rather than split.

Merging Attributes. The opposite approach to the resolution of definition conflicts between attributes is to merge the attributes that overlap and thus create a new attribute with a definition that is broader than the definitions of the merged attributes.

Suppose the entity *reviewer* in the Entity-Relationship Diagram

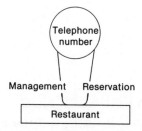

Figure 6.6. Representation of the divided attribute **telephone number**

has two attributes: *name* and *pen name* (Figure 6.7). For each reviewer, we can designate both a real and pen name. When we integrate this diagram with a diagram created for the administration environment, however, we consider these two attributes in light of the attribute *name* as it is assigned to other people who are involved with restaurants. We may decide to merge all the entities representing people who relate to restaurants, as illustrated in Figure 6.5.

But even if we decide to keep *reviewer* as a distinct entity in the integrated schema, it is useful to consider the nature of these two attributes. The attribute *name* as presented in Figure 6.7 has a limited definition: It designates the *real* name of a person. In addition, while a variety of entities have the attribute *name*, very few will have *pen name* attached to them. One way to resolve this conflict is to restrict the definition for the attribute *name* to real names only, and to add the attribute *pen name* to all entities to which it might apply.

This solution, however, is not desirable in the city database. First, it would require a thorough investigation to uncover additional entities for which the distinction between these two types of name is pertinent. We may need to push hard to justify this distinction for other entities, which in turn may result in unnecessary definitional complications. Second, we may discover that this distinction is not essential for reviewers either: Users want

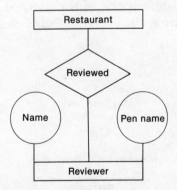

Figure 6.7. A representation of the entity **reviewer** *with two attributes for the name of a reviewer*

to get a review about a restaurant written by a certain person, and whether the name they use for the reviewer is a real name is of no consequence.

In other words, to avoid unnecessary complications and to facilitate a simpler approach to data retrieval by users, we can merge the two attributes *name* and *pen name* into one attribute: *name*. This new attribute includes both real and pen names. A user, asking for a review by a certain reviewer, does not need to know whether the name he enters is a real or a pen name.

Shifting Entities and Attributes. In some instances a definition conflict may occur between an entity and an attribute: An object that is presented in one schema as an entity might be represented in another as an attribute. To resolve such conflicts, we can shift an attribute and change it to an entity, or vice versa.

Consider, for example, the entity *type of food* (see Figure 5.15). We selected this item of data to be an entity in the clientele environment because we wanted to give some information about types of food. We designated in our diagram the average *price* of a certain food type, and a complete database design may give additional information, such as how spicy each type of food is or its nutritional value. In other words, *type of food* is an entity— rather than an attribute—because it has attributes.

It is likely, however, that if "type of food" appears in the administration schema, it would be represented as an attribute of *restaurant*: City officials are not interested in the characteristics of each type of food but may want to know what type of food is served in each restaurant.

In an integrated schema, however, every object is represented either as an entity or as an attribute. Thus a "status" change must be made in one of the schemata. Here it would be sound to change the attribute *type of food* in the administration schema to an entity. Such a change enables us to keep information about the characteristics of types of food for tourists and residents. Integration of the two schemata can then proceed smoothly.

The opposite approach to the resolution of a definition conflict between an entity and an attribute is to shift an entity and change it to an attribute. To illustrate this kind of shift, we use an example from Chapter 5. When we discussed whether an object should be represented as an entity or as an attribute, we examined the entity *grade*, which is given to a restaurant by a reviewer. In Figure 5.13 we relate *restaurant* to *reviewer* through the relationship "reviewed and graded." This relationship also relates *restaurant* and *grade*, and *grade* is related to *reviewer* with the relationship "assigned."

We want to remember here, however, that reviewers are similar to environmental specialists, license officers, or other city personnel—they all examine restaurants, looking for a set of predefined characteristics, and then generate a report and assign a rank of some sort. In addition, it is plausible to assume that the relationship between environmental specialists, for example, and restaurants requires a much simpler representation: the "grade" that such a specialist assigns to a restaurant might be recorded with no mention of the individual specialist who had assigned the grade.

It is useful, therefore, to simplify the network between a reviewer and a restaurant before we integrate the clientele and administration schemata. As shown earlier, shifting the actual object "grade" from an entity to an attribute makes the presentation simpler and more straightforward. In Figure 5.14 the entities *restaurant* and *reviewer* are related by two relationships: "reviewed" and "graded." The relationship "graded" has *grade* as its attribute.

Making "grade" an attribute rather than an entity has various advantages. First, it is more straightforward. Second, it is particularly suitable for representing the relationship between city personnel and restaurants. This can be demonstrated if we substitute the entity *reviewer* for the entity *specialist* or the entity *inspector*. The new configuration separates the examination of a site—using the relationship "reviewed"—and the reporting of findings—using the relationship "graded." This separation is useful because, while some people may perform both processes, others may be involved only in examining a restaurant or in reporting about findings.

We should note here that in this example, shifting *grade* from an entity to an attribute required two other changes. First, the relationship "reviewed and graded" was split into two relationships, each more specific in its definition. Second, the relationship "assigned" was eliminated. While splitting the relationship was our own choice, eliminating the relationship "assigned" was a necessary step once the entity *grade* was removed. The relationship "reviewed and graded" could have remained unaffected because it connects two entities (*grade* and *reviewer*) with the entity *restaurant*; removing one of the entities does not result in the need to eliminate the relationship. The relationship "assigned," on the other hand, represents an association only between the entities *grade* and *reviewer* and, therefore, cannot exist once the entity *grade* is removed.

Conflicts in Inclusion

Inclusion conflicts occur when one schema is "missing" an entity, a relationship, or an attribute that is present in another schema. Such conflicts can usually be resolved by adding a new entity, a new relationship, or a new attribute to the schema.

Adding a New Entity. Entity-Relationship diagrams in two schemata might be almost identical in one of their portions, but one diagram is missing an entity that is represented in the other. For example, the administration schema is likely to include the entity *owner* of a restaurant, which is not represented in the clientele diagram. A simple solution to this discrepancy is to add this entity, as shown in Figure 6.8.

Note that the addition of this entity requires the addition of a

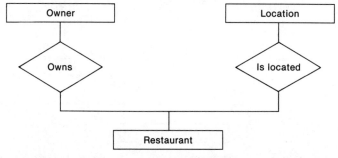

Figure 6.8. Representation of an additional entity: **owner**

new relationship, "owns." The addition of a new entity, though, does not *always* result in the addition of a new relationship. Sometimes new entities can be added to existing relationships.

Adding a New Relationship. The integration of two schemata may require the addition of a relationship to the schema. Fire marshals in the city, for example, may need to know in which neighborhood each owner of an establishment lives so they can determine how soon the owners can get to a site in case of fire. This relationship has not been represented in our diagram so far, but it can be easily added, as shown with the relationship "lives at" in Figure 6.9.

We should note here that the relationship "lives at" was established between two existing entities. In some cases, however, the establishment of a new relationship requires the addition of a new entity.

Adding a New Attribute. The most simple case of inclusion conflicts is when one schema is missing an attribute that is represented in another. When such a conflict occurs, a new attribute is added to the relevant entity or relationship.

Deleting Entities, Relationships, or Attributes. In the previous sections we discussed the modifications that are required to resolve conflicts during schemata integration. These modifications,

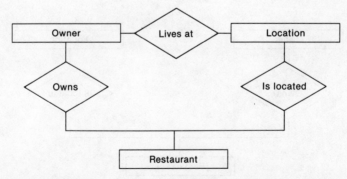

Figure 6.9. Representation of an additional relationship: "lives at"

however, may occur at any stage of the design, and not necessarily as a result of integration. As designers collect more information, and as they progress in the design, they are likely to revise previous decisions and thus introduce modifications.

The set of modifications described here is almost a complete set of modifications possible in the Entity-Relationship Model. To complete this set we need to include the deletion moves: An entity, a relationship, or an attribute may be deleted from a schema. While it is more common to replace rather than delete entities, relationships, or attributes as a result of schemata integration, other procedures in the design of a database require deletion moves.

Some general rules apply to the deletion of elements from a schema. When an entity is deleted all its attributes are also deleted. Moreover, in some instances the deletion of an entity may cause the deletion of a relationship that connects it to other entities. Similarly, when a relationship is deleted, all its attributes are deleted, and the entities to which it is connected may or may not be deleted. In contrast, the deletion of an attribute does not necessitate the deletion of either an entity or a relationship.

DIAGRAM MANAGEMENT

The integration of all the local schemata—and in particular, the local Entity-Relationship diagrams—into a global diagram raises procedural but relevant questions: Where can we find a piece of paper big enough to represent an Entity-Relationship Diagram for a global schema? More seriously, how do we actually lay out the diagram and how do we introduce modifications?

While technical in nature, these questions are important because the Entity-Relationship Model cannot be utilized fully unless a diagram can be drawn. It stands to reason, therefore, that some solutions to these questions have been devised by database designers. Recently, the problem has attracted the attention of researchers who are attempting to find feasible methods for constructing Entity-Relationship diagrams.

Since research focusing on these questions is still in progress, no completely satisfactory solution is yet available. The reader is advised to follow the literature about the Entity-Relationship Model. One way to keep abreast with the developments in this subject area is to participate in an International Conference on the Entity-Relationship Approach. The proceedings of these biannual conferences are usually available to the public, and they too are an important source of information.

The last session in the 1985 Entity-Relationship Conference [2] was dedicated to diagrams and layouts. The papers presented in this session elucidated two approaches to solving layout problems.

One approach is to use only one segment of the diagram at a time. This requires organizing a global schema into subschemata, where each subschemata is reasonably manageable. Here researchers are focusing on useful principles that would guide the partition of a schema into subschemata. In addition, they are investigating what information can be eliminated without affecting the usefulness of the diagram. For example, a designer could draw an Entity-Relationship Diagram in which only entities and relationships are expressed, while attributes are represented only in the data dictionary.

A different approach to the layout problem is to write algorithms for computers to draw Entity-Relationship diagrams. Indeed, some software packages for Entity-Relationship modeling on a microcomputer are available commercially. This approach is particularly convenient because, while the global diagram is stored in the computer, designers can display any portion that is relevant to the issue at hand. At present, a team of scientists at the University of Rome is developing a tool for computer-aided layout of Entity-Relationship diagrams, called GIOTTO. They are investigating general layout criteria for drawing such diagrams based on aesthetic rules.

DATA DICTIONARY UPDATE

As local schemata are integrated to create a temporary global schema, entries in the local, or function-bound, data dictionaries are merged. Thus the temporary data dictionary expands to include additional local data dictionaries. This process terminates when all the local data dictionaries are merged together.

As conflicts are resolved in the integration of schemata, entities, relationships, and attributes are being modified. These modifications should be recorded in the data dictionary. Fortunately, each type of conflict results in a *certain* type of modification. We can, therefore, examine the updating of the data dictionary that is required for each type of conflict.

Before we examine these modifications, however, it is useful to examine again the state of the data dictionary before schemata integration. As illustrated in Figure 4.1, each entry in the data dictionary is for an *item of data*. Items of data are also represented in the Entity-Relationship Diagram. Their representation, however, is more sophisticated: Each item is either an entity or an attribute.

Although the sample data dictionary that we are using would probably have gone through some changes as a result of the construction of the Entity-Relationship Diagram, for simplicity's sake let us assume that the dictionary entries exist as they appear in Figure 4.1. In other words, entities and attributes are represented on cards as items of data, and relationships are not represented at all. Therefore, changes that affect only relationships have no effect on the data dictionary in our discussion here. Similarly, a shift in attributes and entities does not have to be recorded in the data dictionary at this time. In Chapter 7 we describe how to establish entries for relationships and how to distinguish entries for entities from those for attributes. We turn now to the examination of the modifications caused by each type of conflict.

Name Conflicts. Name conflicts occur when the names selected for entities, relationships, or attributes are inconsistent between two schemata. To resolve such conflicts, a designer either modifies the information in dictionary entries or groups together several entries.

Consider the example where the description of the entity *restaurant* in the data dictionary for the function "Going to a restaurant" is different from the one for "Dining in a restaurant." To resolve such a conflict, we should formulate a new description for the entity that fits both functions. In this case, however, we might be better off "clipping together" the two entries for the entity *restaurant* and proceeding further in the integration process, assuming that the inconsistency has been resolved rather then actually formulating the new description.

There are two reasons for postponing the modification of the description. First, we are likely to encounter additional descriptions for the entity *restaurant*. We could, of course, reformulate the description whenever we merge a new restaurant schema. A more efficient way, however, is to collect all the descriptions used in the database and only then, when we can review all the descriptions of the entity *restaurant*, choose a description for the entity that is appropriate for all functions and environments.

Second, as stated earlier, the entity *restaurant* represents the same object for both functions. In other words, we know what we are talking about, and we are consistent in naming it; we only need to describe it better. Under most circumstances we can progress quite far in the design before we need a clear-cut description for this entity.

As is the case with initial descriptions of entities, there are no rules that teach how to reformulate a "good" description for an entity. A designer may feel even more puzzled by the process of creating a description that is appropriate for all functions and environments from a set of descriptions for an entity. The designer has to use all the descriptions collected during integration to formulate a comprehensive description that includes them all.

Frequently, such a task can be achieved by creating a description that is more general, or more abstract, than the original descriptions. Suppose, for instance, that we have three descriptions of *restaurant*: (1) a place where people are served meals for a fee; (2) a place where one can sit and eat; and (3) a place that makes revenues from feeding people. To accommodate all these descriptions, we examine two concepts: the food that is served, and the fee that is charged. Then we attempt to find a more general representation for each one that accommodates the terms used to express these concepts in the three descriptions.

We can say, for instance, that a restaurant is a place that "provides ready-to-eat food." This expression represents a more general concept than "serve meals," "sit and eat," or "feed." Therefore it covers the food-related aspects of the previous descriptions. To further generalize the description, we select a concept to represent the "fee" component. We may describe a restaurant, for example, as a place that "commercially provides ready-to-eat food." This addition covers the fact that a fee is charged and that, for some, a revenue is made.

In contrast to this example, most name conflicts require an immediate revision of the data dictionary. When two distinct entities share the same name—such as the entity *bus*, as previously discussed—a designer must rename the entities to express clearly their differences. We could, for instance, use the name *bus* to represent individual vehicles and call the other entity a *bus route*. When such a conflict is resolved, we must also examine the descriptions of the entities and make sure that they underscore the differences between them.

A different instance of name conflicts occurs when two seemingly distinct entities are actually one and the same. The *cleanliness* of a restaurant and whether it is a *health hazard* are an example of this type of conflict. Clearly, the entries for both attributes should be merged. If it seems that no other attributes are likely to overlap this attribute, a name can be decided on before the global schema is constructed. Otherwise, one may postpone naming the attribute to a later stage. Here again, the description of the newly created attribute is modified to suit the new attribute.

Definition Conflicts. Definition conflicts occur when an entity or an attribute in one schema overlaps an entity in another, but the definitions of the two entities or attributes are not completely identical. Definition conflicts are usually resolved by splitting or merging entities or attributes.

Splitting entities or attributes requires the creation of new entries in the data dictionary. Usually it also results in the elimination of an entity or an attribute.

Consider the example where the entity *person*, which represents all the people in the city administration who relate to restaurants, is split into its components: *inspector, environmental specialist*, and *fire marshal* (see Figure 6.2). Clearly, each of these new entities requires an entry in the data dictionary. These entries should be as complete as possible, with the Synonym and Subset of categories connecting them to other items of data in the data dictionary. The "old" entity, *person*, no longer exists. To be on the safe side, however, we can cross it out but still keep this entry in the dictionary. In addition, it is useful to record on each of the new entries that it is a subset of the entity *person*. This addition shows that the newly created entities are related to one another in some manner.

In addition, this measure of caution is taken to facilitate a smooth reversal of a decision to split an entity. As mentioned before, reversing decisions is not uncommon in database design. It may happen, for instance, that after integrating a few additional schemata with the temporary global schema we realize that a small number of people are in fact involved with restaurants, and each acts in a variety of capacities. We might also discover that users are not interested in the roles people play with relation to restaurants, or in their titles, but rather in the individual persons. Such discoveries call for a merger of the entities representing specific roles to create the entity *person*. The merger can be performed straightforwardly if we have an entry for this "new" entity, and if we can easily trace all the specific entities that compose *person*.

The same procedure can be followed as a result of a split of attributes. In the example about the *name* of a location, two new entries for attributes can be created: *official name* and *common name*. The entry for the attribute *name*, as the entry for any other attribute or entity that has been deleted, is kept until the conceptual schema is completed.

Unlike splitting an attribute, dividing attributes does not require the creation or the deletion of entries from the data dictionary. Rather, it calls for a modification of the description. When the attribute *telephone number*, for example, is divided into *reservation* and *management* numbers, we only have to make sure that the two purposes for which someone may call a restaurant are explicitly delineated in the description. Alternately, we may have a description that is general enough to accommodate for further divisions of the attributes. A description of this attribute, such as "the number to call persons in a restaurant," would also include a direct line to the chef, if needed.

A merger of entities or attributes results in a deletion of entities or attributes and the creation of an entity or an attribute with a more comprehensive definition. For some entities or attributes there is no need to create a new entity or attribute. Consider the previous example of the entity *person* when the entity *reviewer* is merged with it. Here there was no need to create a new entity; we expanded the entity *person* to include restaurant reviewers. At most, we are required to update the description of the expanded entity—and that only if the original description of the entity excludes reviewers.

Inclusion Conflicts. Inclusion conflicts occur when one schema is "missing" an entity or an attribute that is present in another schema. Such conflicts are usually resolved by adding a new entity or attribute.

Adding an entity or an attribute to one schema as a result of integration does not necessarily require any changes in the data dictionary. As the Entity-Relationship diagrams are merged, so are entries in the data dictionaries. Each entity or attribute that is added to the dictionary is checked against the existing ones for consistency and possible relations (synonym, subset of). This process is fundamental to the construction of data dictionaries and is employed from the moment the first entry is established.

The Final Touch. Once all the entries in the data dictionary are updated to correspond with the global Entity-Relationship Diagram, entries for relationships are created and those for entities are separated from entries for attributes. It is best to explain the nature of these "new" entries when rules for entities, relationships, and attributes are illustrated. This is our task in Chapter 7.

SUMMARY

The conceptual schema of a database—which consists of the Entity-Relationship Diagram for the whole database, and the data dictionary—is built by gradually integrating diagrams and entries in the data dictionaries for individual functions, which are called local schemata. The first two local schemata are integrated to establish the temporary global schema that grows gradually as additional local schemata are integrated into it, one by one. The temporary global schema is developed into the global schema when all the local schemata have been integrated.

The procedure of schemata integration is guided by the subject areas and the environments of a database. First, all the local schemata for a subject area within one environment are integrated. Then local schemata for the same subject area within other environments are added, one environment after the other. When the temporary global schema includes all the local schemata for one subject area, the local schemata for the next subject area are integrated into it, one environment after the other.

The process of integrating schemata is one of conflict resolution: The conflicts among entities, relationships, and attributes are explicitly identified and resolved. The nature of the decisions to resolve conflicts is determined by the design specifications of the database.

There are three kinds of conflict: name, definition, and inclusion conflicts. Name conflicts occur when the names selected for entities, relationships, or attributes are inconsistent between two schemata. Inconsistencies of that sort happen when the same name is given to two or more objects that are different or, conversely, when one object is given more than one name. To resolve these conflicts a designer usually changes identical names that are assigned to different objects, or consolidates the names that were assigned to one object.

Definition conflicts occur when an entity in one schema overlaps an entity in another but the definitions of the two are not completely identical. Such conflicts may also occur between relationships or between attributes. These conflicts are usually resolved by splitting entities—breaking one entity type into a number of entity types that are specific in their description—or by merging entities to create a new entity with a definition that is broader than the definitions of the merged entities. Relationships and attributes can also be split or merged to resolve their definition conflicts. In some cases the resolution of a definition conflict requires that entities are changed to attributes or vice versa.

Inclusion conflicts occur when one schema is "missing" an entity, a relationship, or an attribute that is present in another schema. The most common solution to such problems is to add a new entity, relationship, or attribute. Some cases, however, require the deletion of entities, relationships, or attributes. Note that deletion steps should be taken with great caution.

The integration of the local schemata into a global schema may result in an Entity-Relationship Diagram that is too large to be laid out on a single frame. Solutions to this problem are sought in two directions: efficient methods for facilitating the display of portions of the diagram, and computer-aided layout of Entity-Relationship diagrams.

As local schemata are integrated and conflicts are resolved, entries in the data dictionary are modified. The resolution of name conflicts requires either a modification of the information in dictionary entries or a consolidation of several entries. When definition conflicts are resolved, new entries in the data dictionary are frequently created, which, in turn, often result in the elimination of an entity or an attribute. Solving inclusion conflicts, on the other hand, does not always require modifications of entries in the data dictionary.

REFERENCES

1. Chen, P.P.-S. "The Entity-Relationship Model—A Basis for the Enterprise View of Data," in Korfhage, R.R. Ed. 1977. *National Computer Conference, June 13–16, 1977, Dallas, Texas.* Montvale, NJ: AFIPS Press, (AFIPS Conference Proceedings, 46), pp. 77–84. (American Federation of Information Processing Societies).
2. *Proceedings of the 4th International Conference on Entity-Relationship Approach, October 28–30, 1985, Chicago, IL.* Silver Spring, MD: IEEE Computer Society Press, 1985.

7

PREPARATION FOR DATA COLLECTION

With the integrated Entity-Relationship Diagram and the inclusive data dictionary, designers are ready to formulate the rules that are necessary for a consistent and reliable data collection. Entities are actually represented in the database by their identifiers, and attributes by their values that together create a domain for each attribute.

Rules for data collection are of various types, depending on their purpose: (1) rules for occurrence determine whether a relationship, or an attribute, is optional or mandatory; (2) rules for cardinality determine whether a relationship, or an attribute, is one-to-one, one-to-many, or many-to-many; (3) rules for authorized sources define the valid sources of information; (4) rules to establish components in the conceptual schema are necessary when it is not clear whether a particular object or fact "qualifies" as a component; and (5) rules for domains clarify how to select the values pertinent to a specific attribute from among the possible valid values. The rules for each entity, relationship, and attribute are recorded in the data dictionary.

Now that the framework for the database is set, it is time to examine how to represent the data—actual objects, their relationships and attributes. Data collection involves new concepts: entity identifier, attribute value, and attribute domain. In addition, it requires the selection of rules for entities, relationships, and attributes. While these concepts and rules directly relate to a later stage in the construction of a database (when data are actually collected and stored), they are decided on during the design stage.

ENTITY IDENTIFIER

Entities are the objects, or "things," to be represented in a database. What is involved in representing these objects in a database? On the one hand, there are objects, such as the Minaret restaurant, the University District, and the bus running from the University District to downtown, or Mr. Cook (a pen name) who reviews restaurants. On the other hand, a database is a collection of symbols. To represent an entity in a database, a designer "translates" in some manner an object into a string of symbols. Unfortunately, a bus route from the University District to downtown does not have a string of symbols inherent in it, nor does Mr. Cook, the Minaret restaurant, or any other object.

To represent these entities in a database, therefore, one chooses a string of symbols to do the job. A designer could say, for example, that the string of characters "M534" represents the Minaret restaurant. In other words, he would use this string of characters to inform the database that this restaurant is represented. He can also select another string of characters to represent Mr. Cook, say, "C0795," and yet another to represent the bus route.

Thus, for the purposes of entity representation, a string of symbols should be assigned to every entity. Any string of symbols will suffice, as long as it satisfies two conditions:

1. Each string of characters is unique. In other words, every individual entity has one and only one string of symbols to

represent it, and every string of characters represents only one entity.

2. A mechanism exists that makes it easy to find which string of symbols represents which entity, and vice versa. Thus by retrieving a string of characters a designer can easily find what entity it represents; and when he considers an entity, its string of characters is immediately recognizable.

When these conditions are satisfied, the string of symbols that represents an entity is called an *entity identifier*. An entity identifier, then, is the string of symbols that represents an object in a database; one is assigned to each entity so that the database "acknowledges" the entity's representation.

How can entity identifiers be established in an efficient way? Any database is likely to include representations for a very large number of objects in the world. To assign a random string of symbols as an identifier to each entity is a laborious task. A more efficient way to approach the task is to decide what "kind" of identifier should be assigned to entities of the same type. Rather than creating a new and arbitrary string of symbols for each restaurant, for instance, it is much more efficient to have a general rule that determines how to create such an identifier. A rule of that nature states, say, that each restaurant is represented by a code of six letters: The first three are the first three letters in the restaurant's name and the last three signify the type of food.

Thus database designers deal with the issue of entity identifier on the level of *entity type*, rather than on the level of individual entity. Later on, while data are being collected, identifiers for individual entities will be determined according to the rules established here.

The choice of using a general rule to generate entity identifiers, rather than a random or an arbitrary assignment, is supported by other considerations as well. A string of symbols that is randomly selected does not provide any information about the entity it represents. True, an identifier is not supposed to provide information about an entity but merely to represent it in the database. Database designers would, however, save space and effort if they could select identifiers that provide information that they already planned to include in a database.

Consider the entity *location*. To construct an identifier to represent districts and neighborhoods (which are the locations in our database), we could formulate a rule about a location code that is similar to the one we established for restaurants. We may recall, however, that the official name of a location is unique for each location. In other words, each district or neighborhood has only one official name, and no districts or neighborhoods share their official names. Moreover, *official name* is an attribute of the entity *location*. This implies that the official name of each location would be recorded in the database in any event. Because the attribute *official name* satisfies the requirements for an entity identifier—in particular, being unique—it could be used as the identifier for the entity *location*, and no artificial identifier needs to be constructed.

It makes sense to select *official name* as an identifier because locations are in fact *identified* by their names. Therefore this selection is particularly attractive because the more similar the symbols in the database are to conventions of actual usage, the easier the database is to construct and to use.

Such shortcuts are not always possible, though. For instance, to carry this notion to a more general level, one may suggest using the "name" of every entity as its identifier. While this idea is very appealing, one principle should not be forgotten: An entity identifier has to represent an entity *uniquely*. Thus we could not use the *name* of a restaurant as its identifier because two distinct restaurants may share a common name—as in the PauPau case. Alternately, we could not use the *common name* of a location as an identifier because one location may have more than one common name. *Bus number*, on the other hand, is a good identifier for the entity *bus route* because it is a unique identifier, as are other attributes such as the *name* of a *type of food*.

As a general rule we can state, therefore, that any attribute that identifies an entity uniquely is a good candidate for the entity's identifier. Clearly, it is preferable to assign as the identifier an attribute that already exists rather than to create an artificial identifier.

In addition, the second requirement of an identifier—that figuring out which string of symbols represents which entity, and vice versa, is easy—should be given attention. If more than one attribute identifies an entity uniquely, the designer should select the one that best satisfies this condition. In cases where the only attribute that identifies an entity uniquely does not satisfy the second condition, an artificial identifier must be created. Consider, for example, the attribute *telephone number* of an *instance of restaurant*. Suppose that design specifications require that each instance of a restaurant have only one telephone number. Here, a telephone number identifies the entity uniquely. It is not advisable, though, to select it as the identifier of this entity because the notion of identifying restaurants—or establishments of any kind, for that matter—by their telephone number is foreign to most people. There are additional reasons for discarding a *telephone number* as an identifier, as we discuss later.

It is important to note that the second requirement of an identifier should also be satisfied when an artificial identifier is created. While we had to create an artificial code to represent restaurants—a code that is not commonly used—better identifiers can often be selected for other entities. Consider the entity *person*, which represents city personnel who are associated with restaurants. The natural candidate for the identifier here is the Social Security number, commonly used by employers to uniquely identify employees.

These last observations illuminate the nature of entity identifiers, whether selected or especially created: They are attributes of the entities they represent. This revelation should not be surprising; after all, attributes are "pieces" of information about entities, and so are identifiers. For instance, the restaurant code that is assigned to the Minaret restaurant is a piece of information about this restaurant.

Identifiers are represented in the Entity-Relationship Diagram. Figure 7.1 is the Entity-Relationship Diagram that was developed for the function "Going to a restaurant." The identifiers are designated by an additional line, which is curved and broken, between the entity and the identifier.

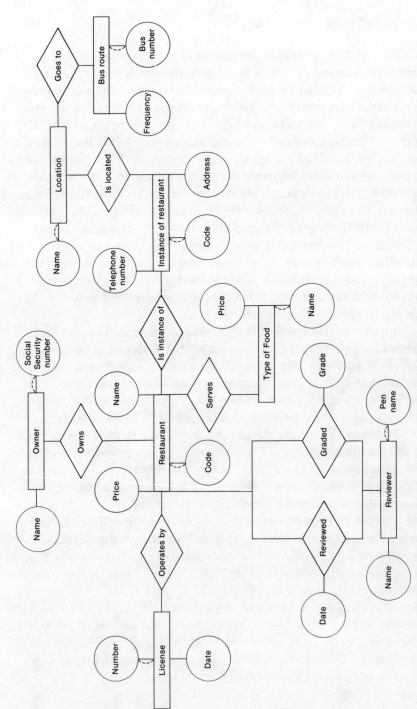

Figure 7.1. Representation of a portion of the Entity-Relationship Diagram for the function "Going to a restaurant" with identifiers

Like any other attribute, entity identifiers require a variety of rules. These rules are discussed in the rest of this chapter where rules for attributes are examined.

ATTRIBUTE VALUES AND DOMAIN

As we have mentioned, in building a database a designer examines objects and facts and represents them with a string of symbols in the database. In other words, attributes of the Minaret restaurant, such as its name, its code, or the range of prices it charges, are each represented with a string of symbols. A string of symbols that represents an attribute of a particular entity is called a *value* of the attribute. Thus "Minaret" is a value of the attribute *name*, "MINMID" is a value of the attribute *code*, and "3-7" is a value of the attribute *price*.

To facilitate an orderly and efficient construction—and operation—of a database, a designer must describe for each attribute what kind of values it can take. An obvious example is the attribute *code* of the entity *restaurant*—which is also the identifier of the entity. No database designer would decide that restaurants are represented by a code without devising an explicit formula to build this code. In other words, this attribute is of help only when the strings of symbols that can represent restaurants are clearly defined. The strings of symbols that can be used to represent an attribute form the *domain* of the attribute.

In more formal language, a domain is a set of values that could be assigned to represent an attribute. From another angle, one may say that the values of an attribute are drawn only from the domain of the attribute. For example, the domain of the attribute *name* might be, "any string of characters." Such a broad definition provides the flexibility needed to record all restaurant names even if they are imaginative and include uncommon symbols. The domain of the attribute *code*, on the other hand, should probably be, "six letters," and that of *price*, "two numbers separated by a hyphen." (Shorter, simpler, and more formal ways to express such domains are discussed in the section "Data Dictionary Entries for Attributes.")

Now that we defined the concepts *entity identifier, attribute values*, and *domain*, we are ready to examine the selection of rules.

THE PURPOSE OF RULES

While entities, relationships, and attributes are described in the data dictionary as comprehensively as possible, experience in database design suggests that actual data collection requires special rules in addition to the general description. The data dictionary description of *type of food*, for example, does not delineate how many types of food a restaurant may have, who has the authority to decide what type of food is served at the Minaret restaurant, or whether Italian food should be recorded as Mediterranean food or just as Italian. Rules are established to answer such questions, thus making the actual representation of objects and facts complete and unambiguous.

How can we find out what rules are needed for the representation of data in a database? If we were to operate in isolation, we would probably have to create the rules as we represent the objects and facts. In other words, every problem encountered during the collection of data would be countered with an appropriate rule. For example, when we first encounter a restaurant in which five distinct types of food are served, we may see the need to limit the number of food types that a restaurant can serve. For that purpose we establish a rule that a restaurant can serve, up to three distinct types of food. Using this procedure, the frequency with which new rules are created would probably decrease as more data are entered, but a complete set of rules would be ready only at the end of data collection.

A better approach is to draw on the experience of other database designers, and to examine the rules they have developed for their databases. Obviously, their rules cannot be directly applied to new databases because they almost always refer to a subject matter and environments that are specific to the database for which they were created. One can, however, analyze what types of questions the rules are supposed to counteract, or what *types* of rules are common to a conceptual schema of a database.

To demonstrate how types of rules can be defined from previous experience, let us examine some possibly knotty points with the entity *owner* of a restaurant—an entity we have not discussed before. Suppose its entry in the data dictionary includes the following description: "the person(s) to which a restaurant belongs." The Minaret restaurant, however, has a peculiar ownership situation: Mr. Latif owns the physical facility, and while he is not involved in any of the restaurant's operations, he receives 10 percent of the profit made. Mr. Haddif, on the other hand, rents the facility (from Mr. Latif, of course), manages the restaurant, and actually collects the profit.

Is Mr. Haddif an owner of the restaurant, or is Mr. Latif? The description of the entity *owner* cannot help us decide because we cannot determine to whom the restaurant *belongs*. Here we face a particular kind of question—How do we determine who is an owner of a restaurant?—and a specific case—when more than one person is qualified as an owner. To solve this problem we can devise a rule that determines who should be considered an owner of a restaurant. For instance, we could state: "If the profit from a restaurant is shared, the person who collects the largest share is considered to be an owner." We assume here that information about shares of profit is available to data collectors because it is included in licensing information.

This modification suggests another question: Can a restaurant have more than one owner? Here again, the description of the entity *owner* in the data dictionary is of no help, and neither is the relationship "owns" because at present there is no information about it. This new question, however, is clearly different in nature from the previous one. There we wanted to determine whether a certain person qualifies to be an owner of a restaurant. Here we ask: Suppose we know how to select rightful owners of restaurants from among several candidates, how many people could be selected as owners of one restaurant? Guided by design specifications, a database designer may decide that there is no limit to the number of restaurant owners, or that there could be only three, or better yet, that only one person can be determined as a restaurant owner. No matter what specific rule is devised, such a question should be answered by the designer before data are collected.

These examples illustrate two types of rules. The first question was: Who qualifies as an owner of a restaurant? Another way to ask this question is: How is the entity *owner* established? This question can be also asked on a more general level: How do we establish an entity? Such a question defines, in turn, the first type of rule: *Rules to establish entities*. In our example we also have a specific case in which the problem occurs: More than one person qualifies as an owner. Here we can be more precise in defining the type of rule and explicitly mention a problematic case for establishing entities: when more than one object qualifies as an entity.

The second type of rule is illustrated by the question: How many owners can one restaurant have? As illustrated earlier, this question can be asked on a more general level: How many entities in an entity type can be related through a relationship to *one* entity in another entity type? This formulation may now seem somewhat awkward, but we will return to it later when we discuss the cardinality of relationships.

It should be noted that while a designer must be aware of the *types* of rules that are pertinent to each entity, relationship, or attribute, he should not insist on creating his own rules. In fact, to apply rules that are already used by the environment as much as possible is a requirement for a good design. Rules to determine, for instance, how many owners a restaurant can have, probably have been devised already by the legal department of the city. The department might have even established a procedure to determine who the owner of each restaurant is. Because the entity *owner* is of prime relevance to city officials, and probably of little interest to the clientele, the rules issued by the legal department should be applied in the database design. To discover such rules, however, a designer must first raise the questions, How many owners can a restaurant have, and who can qualify as an owner of a restaurant? In other words, an examination of the types of rules is the safest way for discovering rules and guidelines already in use that are pertinent to the database design.

Ideally, during the construction of the conceptual schema all

the problems that will be encountered in data collection are anticipated, and rules to resolve them devised. In this way the creation
of rules can progress in a systematic and consistent manner, and
the conceptual schema need not be constantly updated. Obviously, however, this ideal is unrealistic: No matter how well one
is prepared for data collection, some unanticipated problems
arise. A list of the types of rules, though, is extremely useful because it can be used as a guide to anticipating problems, thus
increasing a designer's ability to devise rules for anticipated problems.

Suppose one clarifies the types of rules used in one database,
how can these types be used to generate rules pertinent to a new
database?

To demonstrate how a list of rule types is used, let us consider
the two types of rules mentioned earlier. Suppose we are examining the entity *type of food*. To use the rule types, we check whether
or not they are applicable to the entity. The first rule type predicts
that we may have problems in establishing this entity, and in particular when more than one object can be selected as an entity.
Now we ask ourselves: What are examples of situations in which
two or more "things" compete among themselves to qualify as
type of food?

One example that comes to mind is the case of a creative restaurant owner. As you recall, our data dictionary defines *type of food*
by owners of restaurant: Whatever they claim to be the type of
food they serve is designated as a type of food. We should anticipate, however, that some owners, in an attempt to attract customers, will claim to serve unique types of food—such as, "green
food" or "energy food."

How would we handle such types of food when we encounter
them? We could, of course, follow the broad definition that is
coined in the data dictionary, accept these terms as types of food,
and discard the whole matter. If we wish to be more rigorous,
however, we should examine the matter more closely. It makes
sense to assume (so we speculate) that green food is actually vegetarian food, and energy food is nothing but health food. Therefore, we maintain, these new and creative names should be controlled and changed into a more conventional form. To
accommodate for such a control, we can devise a rule such as: "If

a type of food is based on *one* type of ingredient, the type of food is determined by its ingredients." Thus, when collecting data about types of food, one should check each of the types given by restaurant owners to determine whether any could be named after the ingredients involved.

The second type of rule is much simpler. It gives rise to the question, How many types of food can one restaurant have? We can decide whether to limit the number of types of food that are recorded for each restaurant. The rule type is helpful here, though, because it explicitly refers us to this question and reminds us to devise a pertinent rule.

As these examples illustrate, a list of the types of rules that have been used in the design of databases is helpful in the establishment of rules for entities, relationships, and attributes in a new database. This chapter brings together types of rules that have been used in the design of bibliographic databases. It is based in particular on the Anglo-American Cataloging Rules [1]. While the actual cataloging rules are not mentioned here, the types of rules they create are presented and their applications to the city database are illustrated with examples.

RULES FOR OCCURRENCE

The relationships in an Entity-Relationship Diagram represent associations among entities that are relevant to the performance of the functions that the database is supposed to support. Therefore the entities *restaurant* and *type of food*, for example, are connected by the relationship "serves." This relationship indicates that restaurants by themselves—or types of food by themselves—are of little relevance to the potential users; they need to know *which* restaurant serves *what* types of food. Differently put, users may ask what type of food is served in a restaurant of their choice, or they may want to know which restaurant serves their favorite type of food.

If one examines the nature of relationships on the level of individual entities—rather than on the entity-type level—one can imagine a list of restaurants with the food types each serves, or a list of types of food, and for each the restaurants in which it is served.

With that image of lists, we can easily understand the concept of *occurrence*. Rules that determine the occurrence of a relationship answer the question, Does every restaurant serve at least one type of food? Or, Is every type of food served by at least one restaurant? An occurrence rule states whether a relationship is mandatory or whether it is optional; whether the relationship occurs for each and every individual entity or whether it occurs for some entities but not for others.

In our example, we may conclude that we are required to accommodate situations in which a certain restaurant serves food that is of no particular type. Under such conditions, the relationship "serves" is optional. Alternately, we may decide that each restaurant has to serve some type of food, regardless of how specific this type is. In this case the relationship is mandatory, and later we would have to formulate rules to determine what *type of food* is served in restaurants that do not really serve any particular type of food.

While the relationship "serves" allows designers to make decisions about its occurrence, other entities leave creators of conceptual schemata no choice. Consider, for example, the relationship "goes to" between the entities *location* and *bus route*. No matter what the design specifications for a database are, each bus goes to a certain location, and this relationship is therefore always mandatory. In contrast, some locations may not be on a busline, and the relationship in the other direction—"can be reached by"—is optional.

Attributes resemble relationships because they associate a "piece" of information with an object. The attribute *name*, for example, provides no information unless it is associated with an entity, such as *restaurant* or *reviewer*. Thus, because attributes implicitly represent associations, their occurrence needs to be explicitly specified.

The occurrence of an attribute may or may not be predetermined. A *reviewer*, for instance, may or may not have a *pen name*. A database designer is free to decide whether this attribute is optional or mandatory. If optional, this attribute is not recorded for reviewers who lack a pen name. If mandatory, however, the designer needs to formulate a rule to determine what values to record for reviewers with no pen names. One possibility, for example, is to record the name they use to sign their reviews, whether it is a pen name or a real name.

The occurrence of other attributes is predetermined and the role of a designer is to recognize this occurrence and to record it. It makes sense to assume here that each restaurant has an address, and each bus runs in some designated frequency. The attributes *address* of *restaurant* and *frequency* of *bus route* are therefore mandatory. But so are *restaurant's code* and the *official name* of *location*. These attributes are identifiers; they represent entities and therefore have values whenever an entity is represented. In other words, *the occurrence of identifiers is always mandatory*.

The occurrence of each relationship or attribute is recorded both on the Entity-Relationship Diagram and in the data dictionary. On the Entity-Relationship Diagram, only optional relationships or attributes are designated as such. A slash across the line connecting a relationship or an attribute with the entity for which it is optional designates the optional occurrence, as illustrated in Figure 7.2. Data dictionary entries for relationships and attributes are discussed in the section "Data Dictionary Entries."

RULES FOR CARDINALITY

The cardinality of a relationship determines how many individual entities in an entity type can be associated with *one* entity in the other entity type, and vice versa. Examples include how many types of food one restaurant can serve, and how many restaurants serve one type of food; or, how many owners one restaurant can have, and how many restaurants one person can own.

The cardinality of relationships can be expressed as one of three options:

1. *One-to-One Relationship (1:1).* One entity of a type can be associated with only one entity of another type, and vice versa. The relationship "operates by"—which associates *restaurant* with *license*—is an example of that kind of cardinality: Each restaurant

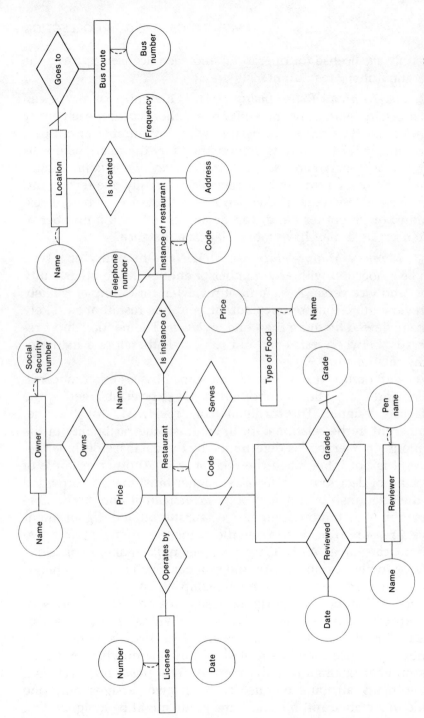

Figure 7.2. Representation of a portion of the Entity-Relationship Diagram for the function "Going to a restaurant" with occurrence of relationships and attributes

161

has only *one* license for operation, and each license approves the operation of *one* restaurant.

2. *One-to-Many Relationship (1:M).* One entity of a type can be associated with only one entity of another type but each entity of the other type can be associated with any number of entities. This kind of relationship is demonstrated by the relationship "is instance of"—between *restaurant* and *instance of restaurant*. An instance of a restaurant can be associated with only one restaurant, the "parent" restaurant of which it is an instance. A parent restaurant, on the other hand, can be associated with a number of instances, as it may have more than one instance.

3. *Many-to-Many Relationship (M:N).* One entity of a type can be associated with any number of entities in the other entity type, and vice versa. A restaurant reviewer, for example, is likely to review more than one restaurant, and one restaurant is likely to be reviewed by more than one reviewer. The relationship "reviewed" between *restaurant* and *reviewer* is therefore a many-to-many relationship.

As with occurrence, some relationships possess inherent cardinality, and the cardinality of others needs to be established by the database designer. The cardinality of "reviewed" for example, is inherent in the relationship. In contrast, the cardinality of the relationship "serves" is determined by the database designer because it is not inherent in the relationship. Another example of the kind of decisions a database designer must make is provided by the relationship "owns," between *restaurant* and *owner*. One person may own more than one restaurant, but a designer might have a reason to restrict to one the number of owners that a restaurant can have. A database designer must make a conscious choice whether or not to limit the number. Such a decision determines the cardinality of the relationship "owns."

The cardinality of an attribute designates how many values of the attribute can be assigned to one individual entity, and vice versa. The attribute *number* of the entity *bus route* is a one-to-one attribute because each bus route has only one number, and each bus number belongs to only one bus. The *grade*, however, is a one-to-many attribute because each reviewer assigns only one grade to a restaurant, but the same grade might be assigned to a number of restaurants or to the same restaurant by a number of reviewers. In contrast, the *price* of food in a *restaurant* is a many-to-many attribute because a restaurant may charge more than one price range, and a certain price range can be charged by a number of restaurants.

As with occurrence, some attributes possess inherent cardinality, and the cardinality of others needs to be established by the database designer. He must decide whether to limit the number of telephones a restaurant can have to one—and thus establish it as a one-to-one attribute—or whether to record all the telephone numbers a restaurant might have. The *date* on which a restaurant was "reviewed" by a certain *reviewer*, however, is predetermined to be single-valued, and a number of restaurants might be reviewed in the same day by a number of reviewers. In other words, the cardinality of the attribute *date* of the relationship "reviewed" is predetermined.

Note, however, that *the cardinality of entity identifiers is always one-to-one.* For the identifier to be unique, it must have the cardinality of one-to-one.

Examining the occurrence and the cardinality of entity identifiers, we may conclude that an identifier is always a one-to-one and mandatory attribute. It is also safe to say that *almost every attribute that is one-to-one and mandatory can serve as the identifier of the entity it describes.* Using this generalization, we can explain why, for instance, a *telephone number* cannot serve as an identifier, even if a restaurant is limited to only one telephone number: Its occurrence is not mandatory, as some restaurants may not have a telephone. Incidentally, another reason for not selecting the *telephone number* as an identifier—and a realistic one—is that these numbers change fairly often.

The cardinality of each relationship and attribute is recorded on the Entity-Relationship Diagram, as shown in Figure 7.3. It is also recorded in the data dictionary, as discussed in the section "Data Dictionary Entries."

RULES FOR AUTHORIZED SOURCES

A special set of rules must be created to determine which sources of information to consult about entities, relationships, or attributes. For example, what sources of information should be con-

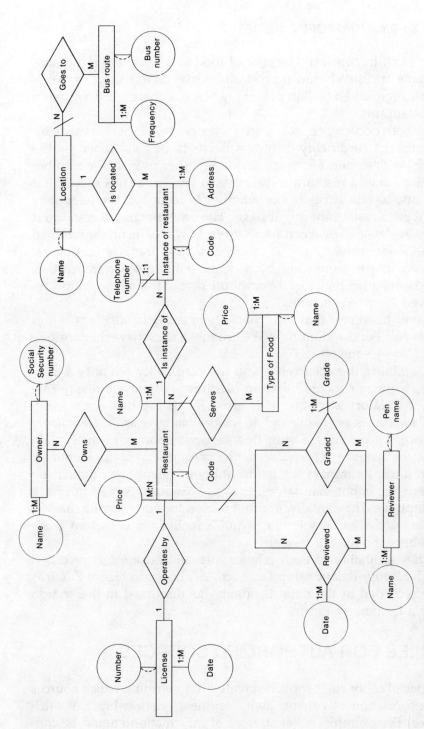

Figure 7.3. Representation of a portion of the Entity-Relationship Diagram for the function "Going to a restaurant" with occurrence and cardinality of relationship and attributes

sulted to determine who is an owner of a restaurant? Should we ask the person who runs the restaurant, the restaurant's employees, or should we examine the city records? Obviously, the same type of source should be used to determine ownership of all restaurants in the database. Therefore, we want to devise a rule that states clearly which sources can be used.

Rules for authorized sources are of three types:

1. A general rule that states the authorized source of information

2. A rule for entities, relationships, or attributes that lack the authorized source

3. A rule for entities, relationships, or attributes that have more than one authorized source.

General Rules

A general rule usually appears at the beginning of a set of rules; it clearly states the authorized source of information. This statement can take two forms. Either a database designer selects one, and only one, source as the authorized source of information, or he decides that *any* source will do. In other words, the general rule either designates *the* source of information, or it states that there are no specially authorized sources.

For instance, to achieve a reliable design, a designer should pick an "authority" that would provide the information about the type of food that is "served" in a restaurant. It also makes sense to decide that the menu of a restaurant is the best source for information about the food served. Therefore, a rule for the authorized source for the relationship "served" would probably be: "Collect data about the type of food that a restaurant serves from its menu." Other examples of such a general rule are: "Record the license number from the license itself" and "Use the telephone directory as the authorized source for telephone numbers."

In contrast, a designer may decide that information concerning *type of food* can be collected from any "knowledgeable" source.

In other words, while *type of food* is defined as the type that the owner claims to serve, one does not necessarily have to ask the owner himself; the chef, the employees, regular diners, or even the sign in the window can clarify what type of food the owner claims to serve. Note here that whether or not a particular type is *actually* served in a restaurant is a different issue, which is discussed later when rules for establishing the relationship "serves" are examined.

Attributes may yet require a special form of a general rule, a rule for dependent authorized sources. Such a rule states that the authorized source of information for an attribute is determined by the authorized source that is used to establish the entity which it describes. For example, rather than specifying the authorized source for the *name* of a *location*, one can state: "Names of locations should be taken from the authorized source that is used to establish the entity *location*." This kind of a rule covers instances in which the source is not available, or those in which there are more than one source.

Lack of Authorized Sources

If the general rule designates a *single* authorized source of information, a database designer must devise a rule of the second type—a rule for entities, relationships, and attributes that lack such a source. Some restaurants, for example, may not have a menu—such as the Ham & Egg restaurant, which is a one-person operation—and thus raise difficulties in determining what type of food is served. Similarly, the telephone number of a restaurant may not be listed in the directory.

Rules for entities, relationships, or attributes that lack the authorized source of information can take two forms. First, one may state: "If the authorized source of information is lacking, use *any* source of information." Thus, to determine what type of food is served at the Ham & Egg restaurant, a database designer may interrogate any person she wishes.

The second option takes a more cautious approach: Here the rule provides a list of other sources that can be used, which may even be organized in an order of preference. Thus one may instruct: "If the telephone number of a restaurant is not listed in the directory, consult the manager or an advertisement for the restaurant in a newspaper." Another rule may state the alternate sources in a ranked order: "If a restaurant has no menu, accept information about the type of food it serves from (a) waiters; (b) chef; (c) manager; (d) owner; and (e) diners."

Multiple Authorized Sources

An individual entity, relationship, or attribute may have more than one authorized source of information. Here the third type of rule applies. For a reliable collection of data, a database designer should solve such a problem by designating additional criteria that would determine how an authorized source of information should be selected.

As we formulate authority rules for the relationship "serves," for instance, we want to consider the case of a restaurant having more than one menu. One database designer may decide that such a situation is highly unlikely and dismiss the case. Another designer may decide to be more cautious and be prepared even for the virtually impossible. This designer then applies two criteria: "If a restaurant has more than one menu, consult the menu printed most recently; and if all menus were printed at the same time, consult the one that includes the largest number of dishes."

ESTABLISHING ENTITIES, RELATIONSHIPS, AND ATTRIBUTES

Rules to establish entities, relationships, and attributes guide data collection concerning whether a particular object "qualifies" as a specific entity, a relationship exists among objects, or a particular fact should be recorded as an attribute of a particular entity. These are the rules that a person who collects data should consult when examining an object or fact if he is having difficulty deciding whether the object belongs to a certain entity type or attribute and how it should be associated with other entities or attributes.

Three conditions require such rules:

1. When subtle issues need to be emphasized or the description of an entity, relationship, or attribute requires some elaboration

2. When several objects could qualify as entities, a few associations as a relationship, or a number of facts as an attribute, all to varying degrees—the case of fuzzy entities, relationships, or attributes

3. When an object can be defined either as one entity or another, an association as one relationship or another, or a fact as one attribute or another—the borderline case

Elaboration Rules

Elaboration rules add checking points that can be used at data collection to double check whether a particular entity, relationship, or attribute is established "correctly." Such rules can either state facts that are already known, thus providing for clarification, easy consistency checks, and emphasis of subtle points; or they may provide a checklist.

Elaboration rules that aim at clarification anticipate possible misconceptions and emphasize subtleties. An example of such a rule for the entity *license* is, "A license to operate a restaurant must be given by the City's License Department. Licenses issued by licensing departments of other cities should be ignored."

Some such elaboration rules highlight readily available check points for consistency. For example, to help in recording objects for the entity type *instance of restaurant*, one may state, "an instance of a restaurant has the same name as the restaurant of which it is an instance." While such a rule does not add any information, it facilitates a mechanism for easy detection of mistakes or inconsistencies. Another example of such a rule is the statement "a location must have a name that corresponds to a designated location in the Official District Map issued by the City."

Relationships may also need elaboration rules of that type. To increase consistency in collecting data about the relationship "graded," for example, one may state the rule, "If a reviewer has 'graded' a restaurant, he or she has also 'reviewed' the restaurant. Similarly, the relationship "operates by"—which associates the entities *license* and *restaurant*—may require a rule such as "a restaurant 'operates by' a license only if the license has a number and an expiration date."

In the same fashion, elaboration rules can serve as a reminder and an easy check for errors. A designer could decide, for example, that "only an *instance of a restaurant* can be related to a *location*—the headquarters of a chain of restaurants has no location unless it is also an instance of a restaurant"; or, "a bus 'goes to' all the locations on its route."

The attribute *grade* provides another example of an elaboration rule that aims at clarification. For instance, even it if is clearly stated that the authorized source of information for the attribute *grade* that a *reviewer* assigned to a *restaurant* is the published review, a designer could add a rule such as: "Record the grade assigned by a reviewer to a restaurant in the text of the review; do not record a grade that was communicated to you in any other manner."

The other form of elaboration rules, the checklists, are useful for some entity types or attributes. Consider, for example, the entity *reviewer* of restaurants. While the description of this entity type in the data dictionary might be simple—for instance, a person who makes his or her review of a restaurant known to the public—individual "reviewers" may raise some questions. For example, is a person who regularly writes reviews of restaurants in which he dines, and makes his reviews available to his friends, a reviewer? Is a person who wrote a review for her high school alumni newsletter about a restaurant opened by an alumna of the school a reviewer? Surely there are many other examples of people who write restaurant reviews but are not exactly restaurant reviewers.

To provide for a clear distinction between persons who just write restaurant reviews and those who are "truly" reviewers, we could have constructed a set of rules that would set the record straight for each person. Such a task, however, is likely to require much time, as it involves speculations about a large variety of instances in which persons who write reviews are not restaurant reviewers in the strict sense. In such a case, we may want to examine first how many people qualify as reviewers. Running a quick check, we may find that about 15 restaurant reviewers work in the city. This number suggests that we consider a checklist. We can simply list the top 15 reviewers in the city—thereby establishing a Reviewers List—and formulate the elaboration rule: "A person is a reviewer only if her or his name is on the Reviewers List."

Checklists require constant updating, but a list limited to the top 15 people would change less often. In addition, the advantages of this approach are clear: The checklist is relatively short and easy to skim, and the person who collects the data is saved from "testing" each potential reviewer against an elaborate set of rules. Similarly, to secure the consistency of the attribute *grade*, one may formulate the rule: "Record a grade only if it appears in the text of the review in the form: poor, fair, good, very good, or excellent." The list of grades is very short and is not likely to require updating.

Another example of the checklist approach can be illustrated with the entity *location*. Suppose restaurant owners are the source of information for restaurant locations—an authorized source for the relationship "is located." Mr. Haddif, the owner of the Minaret restaurant, informs Sue, who is collecting data, that his restaurant is located in the Triangle. Sue knows that the Triangle refers to a group of buildings downtown, but she has to decide whether or not it is a legitimate location. To aid her with such a decision, we can provide the Official District Map of the city, on which neighborhoods and districts are clearly marked. A rule to follow in this case might be: "Identify the place in which a restaurant is located in the Official District Map and record the designated district as the location." Here, the Official Map serves as a checklist.

Fuzzy Entities, Relationships, or Attributes

Fuzzy Entities. The most common occurrence of fuzzy entities is when a number of objects could qualify as an entity, some more so than others. Here a rule must be devised that provides additional criteria for establishing entities.

Let us consider again the entity *reviewer* of a restaurant. We have already seen that the description of this entity type in the data dictionary may raise questions when individual "reviewers" are examined. In the previous section we assumed that the number of reviewers is relatively small and unchanging and proposed therefore to establish a Reviewers List.

Suppose, however, that such assumptions cannot be made. Here we encounter a typical fuzzy case: A great number of people may qualify as reviewers, and some more so than others. Clearly, one must formulate a rule—or possibly a set of rules—to facilitate a correct selection of reviewers. Assuming that the description in the data dictionary is "a person who makes his/her review of a restaurant known to the public," rules of various forms can be devised.

The most straightforward way to resolve this fuzziness is to devise explicit criteria to determine when a review was actually made known to the public. Here a designer may select a general statement, such as "a person is a reviewer if his/her reviews appeared in a publication that has a circulation of at least 5,000." Alternately, a designer may state the publications that are "qualified" as sources of information to the public: "A person is a reviewer if his or her reviews have been published in major daily or weekly newspapers and magazines, or in books about restaurants." If needed, one could even list some of the publications by name.

Another method to resolve a fuzzy case—which might or might not be used with other rules—is to provide additional criteria for the selection of a reviewer. An example of such a rule is: "A person qualifies as a reviewer if he has published at least 10 restaurant reviews in the last year and if the reviews have been published on a regular basis."

The entity type *reviewer* may also require criteria for special situations. In writing rules for this entity we may want to consider, for instance, Mr. Feinschmecker—a retired art critic who is well known and admired for the occasional restaurant reviews he publishes in a local newspaper. Because of his reputation we would like to consider him as a reviewer and include his reviews in the database. To accommodate for such special cases one can create a rule such as: "A person who publishes reviews in publications with low circulation, or not on a regular basis, qualifies as a reviewer if he or she is well known as a reviewer."

In contrast, a designer may want to specify that other criteria are of no consequence in the determination of the entity *reviewer*. An example of such a rule is: "A person qualifies as a reviewer regardless of how popular his or her reviews are, whether or not writing restaurant reviews is the main source of his or her income, and regardless of the degree to which this person is knowledgeable about food."

Fuzzy Relationships. Rules for fuzzy relationships are consulted when it is not clear whether a case qualifies as a relationship, or when some cases qualify as a relationship more than others. These rules are likely to constitute one of the largest sets of rules in a database, because they define under what conditions each relationship holds.

What are the kinds of problems that require the use of rules for fuzzy relationships? Let us consider again the relationship "serves" that relates the entities *restaurant* and *type of food*. For this purpose, let us also assume that it is a mandatory, many-to-many, relationship. That is, each restaurant *must* have a food type assigned to it, and each type of food is served in at least one restaurant; and also a restaurant can serve more than one food type, and a type of food can be served in more than one restaurant.

First, relationships that cannot be ascertained straightforwardly require rules that specify the criteria to use—or the procedure to follow—to establish them. For instance, to ascertain whether or not license number 5428 authorizes the operation of the Minaret restaurant, a designer can check if the name of the restaurant is printed on the license. The general rule to establish this relationship is very simple: "Check the name on the license." To determine whether this restaurant serves Italian food, however, is a little more complex. This relationship requires a rule such as: "The type of food that a restaurant serves is determined by the following procedure: each dish on the menu is assigned a type of food; the types of food are then ranked by number of dishes, eliminating types for which less than four dishes are available. The first three on the list are selected as the types of food."

Second, one-to-many or many-to-many relationships may require that the number of objects in an entity type that correspond to one object in another be limited. Therefore, a database designer should examine each relationship and determine whether such a limitation should be imposed. For the "serve" relationship, we may decide that while a type of food can be served in any number of restaurants, a restricting rule should be created for restaurants: "A restaurant can serve up to three distinct types of food."

Third, it may happen that a relationship that is mandatory cannot be established for a particular entity. A rule about how to "establish" a relationship in such cases should be devised. A restaurant, for example, may not have a distinct type of food to offer because the number of dishes it serves of each food type is smaller than four. A database designer should anticipate such a case and create a rule similar to: "If there is no evidence that a restaurant serves a specific type of food, assign 'general' as its type of food."

Similarly, we may end up with types of food in our list that are not assigned to any restaurant. The relationship "serves," however, is mandatory and we must therefore create a rule to accommodate such discrepancies. An example of such a rule is: "If a type of food has not been associated with a restaurant, using the procedure of menu examination, assign it to the restaurant that serves the largest number of its dishes."

Fourth, a rule should be formulated to guide decisions in case of doubt. Such rules may suggest additional examinations, or they may instruct whether to give a relationship the benefit of doubt. For example, "In case of doubt whether or not a restaurant serves a particular type of food, assign this type of food to the restaurant."

Fifth, it may happen that the source of information with which one consults, and the procedures one follows to establish a relationship, lead to erroneous results. One may know, for instance, that the license to operate the Hall restaurant is about to be suspended. Yet, if no rule exists to guide data collection in such cases, one would probably follow the authorized source—which is probably the license itself—and record the license number and expiration date, as if the restaurant were operated by the license. Other data collection personnel may decide to designate that the restaurant has no license—an approach that would serve the interests of city personnel. Such inconsistency in data collection is unacceptable to an alert database designer, who is likely to provide a rule that explicitly states: "A license that is about to be suspended should not be recorded." Other relationships, however, may require different instructions. Anticipating a similar instance with the relationship "serves," for example, one may create a rule such as: "Even if it is known that some dishes of a certain type of food are not actually served, select it as a type of food if it scores high enough."

Last, one-to-one relationships or one-to-many relationships should be protected against instances in which an entity that is supposed to relate to only one entity from another type actually relates to more than one entity. A rule must be created that determines whether to split the original entity, or whether to select one among the entities that can possibly relate to it.

The relationship "operates by" is a relevant example here. A database designer must anticipate instances in which a restaurant has more than one license even though it is supposed to have only one license. Design specifications and requirements on the entity *restaurant* determine which rule to select. For one database a designer may create a rule that allows for the restaurant being split into a number of restaurants, each corresponding to a license. Alternately, he may devise the rule: "If a restaurant has more than one license, record the earliest one."

Fuzzy Attributes. As illustrated with examples for entities and relationships, rules for fuzzy attributes are important when a number of facts could qualify as an attribute, and some more so than others. Examples of a few instances of fuzzy attributes are discussed here.

The first example is the use of additional criteria to select the "right" attribute when more than one fact qualifies as an attribute. If, for example, the *name* of a *reviewer* is a one-to-many attribute, a designer may want to anticipate the unlikely case in which a reviewer has more than one name. Here, a rule that specifies additional criteria for determining a reviewer's name is of help, such as: "If a reviewer has more than one name, use the one by which he is most commonly known."

Second, a rule for a fuzzy attribute may dictate a procedure to determine a value for the attribute. Consider the question of how to determine the price range of a restaurant. A database designer may prescribe the following procedure: "Examine the prices on the menu for dishes that are not appetizers nor desserts. The price range starts with the second lowest price on the list (unless there are at least three dishes available in the lowest price), and concludes with the highest price on the list for which at least two dishes are available."

This procedure reminds us of a third example: a rule that determines how to "establish" an attribute that is mandatory but cannot be established. The attribute *price* is mandatory; yet, following the above procedure, we may not be able to establish a price range for a restaurant that serves only desserts, or for a restaurant in which the prices change every night according to the daily special. To facilitate data collection in such problematic instances, one may formulate a rule: "If the price of food at a restaurant cannot be determined using the designated procedure, ask the manager to quote the range of price." Note that this rule probably requires the use of a source of information other than the authorized one.

Rules for fuzzy attributes can also guide data collection in case of doubt, or when the information found in the authorized source is known to be incorrect. An example of a rule that provides instructions in case of doubt is: "Enter a common name of a location that is taken from a valid source of information even if it is not completely clear whether or not the name is in common use." Incorrect information may also be entered in some cases. To ensure that a *name* is entered for each *reviewer*, for example, a rule can be formulated that states: "If the name found in the authorized source for a reviewer is incorrect, enter it if the correct name is unknown; otherwise, enter the correct name."

Last, a one-to-many or many-to-many attribute may require a limit on the number of values that can be assigned to each entity. One may state, for example, "A restaurant can have no more than three price ranges."

Borderline Cases

Rules for borderline cases must be formulated to accommodate instances in which an object can be defined either as one entity or another. For each entity type, we should try to predict such instances and determine whether such objects should be recorded as two distinct entities, or whether one entity type is preferred to the other and under what conditions.

The entity types *restaurant* and *instance of restaurant* provide a relevant example. It is probable that many restaurants recorded in a database have only one instance. In other words, many of them serve certain types of food, charge prices of a certain range, and are located in one place only. When examining the Minaret restaurant—which is an example of such a restaurant—one may wonder whether it is a *restaurant* or an *instance of a restaurant*. Following the descriptions for these two entity types, it is clear that the Minaret restaurant is both. To ensure that every person who collects data follows these descriptions accurately, we may add a rule for both entity types: "If a restaurant has only one instance of a restaurant, the restaurant is recorded both as a *restaurant* and as an *instance of a restaurant*."

For other entity types a clear separation may be more suitable. An example is the rule: "A shopping center that houses more than 20 establishments is considered as a *location*; otherwise it is recorded as an *address*." Such a rule requires that a shopping center be recorded only once and provides the conditions that determine its entity type. Thus the street address of a restaurant in South Central Mall would not include the name of the mall, which will be recorded as its location. The address of a restaurant in the Small Neighborhood Mall, on the other hand, would include the name of the mall, and its location would be the specific neighborhood.

Rules for establishing attributes are also necessary for borderline cases, when a fact can be defined either as one attribute or as another. Here again, such a rule determines whether the fact is recorded as two attributes, or whether it is considered as one attribute and under what conditions.

An example of a borderline case is a *location* for which the official name and the common name are one and the same. A database designer may instruct that in such a case, the name be recorded as both the *official name* and the *common name* attributes. Or, he may decide that it is important to record a common name only when it is different from the official name; otherwise a location simply does not have a common name.

RULES FOR DOMAINS

The domain defines the valid values that each attribute can have. It does not explain, however, how to select from among the possible valid values, the values pertinent to an attribute of a *particular* entity. Rules for the domain are created for that purpose. For instance, while the domain of a restaurant *code* is a string of six letters, only a rule can explain how to construct the code for the Minaret restaurant. The most common type of rule here is the general rule, which is required for the domains of most attributes. In addition, the domain of some attributes calls upon rules for fuzzy domains.

General Rules

These rules give instructions about the construction and selection of values for attributes of individual entities. The most common type of a general rule is the *basic* rule, which provides the most general instructions about how to select values. Consider the attribute *address* of a restaurant—or of an *instance of a restaurant*, to be more precise. Suppose the authorized source of information for this attribute, as is discussed later, is the restaurant's license because it is very unlikely that it would be recorded incorrectly. An example of a basic rule for the domain of the attribute *address* is: "Record the address of a restaurant exactly as it appears on the restaurant's license." Thus the street address of the Minaret restaurant is copied from the license as "University Ave." even though the official name of the street now is "University Way."

Suppose, however, that a database designer thinks that addresses are recorded on licenses in an inconsistent manner: Some include postal box numbers and others do not; for some restaurants only the street address is given, for others only the name of the shopping center in which they are located is recorded; and yet for others both appear on the license, and so on. While retaining the restaurant license as the authorized source of information, the designer may prefer then to state—in a rule—what parts of the address to record. Such a rule is a *content* rule: It states what information to include in the values for each attribute.

The designer could establish a list of elements to be included in the value for an address, such as number, street, city, and zip code. Still another form of such a rule is to require that, at the minimum, these four elements be recorded and additional information be added, if relevant. While a content rule can take one of these two forms, it is important to verify its consistency with the basic rule. One would like to avoid a situation in which, say, an element that is required to be recorded as a value of *address* is never listed on the license.

General rules must be formulated in anticipation of a variety of exceptions and irregularities. Some examples of such irregularities and the rules they require are given below.

The first example is the *missing-value* rule. Its purpose is to provide guidance about the selection of a value when the collector knows that a value exists but is unable to find it. For instance, one may not be able to find the real name of Mr. Cook, who is a restaurant reviewer. According to the data dictionary, however, the attribute *name* of the entity *reviewer* is mandatory. This means that the *name* of Mr. Cook must have a value. A strict database designer may not accept a missing value and may require the value to be found—in fact, for some attributes this choice might be a necessity. A more flexible designer may accommodate for missing values and create the rule: "If the real name of a reviewer cannot be ascertained, enter 'unknown.'" Here, the term unknown is a valid value for the attribute *name* of a *reviewer*. A similar rule may suggest entering a pen name, assuming those are always available. A designer should ensure, however, that this rule is consistent with the rules for establishing the attribute *name*.

Another example are domains for attributes that accept more than one value for a single entity; they may require a *sequence* rule, or a rule that explains in what order these values be recorded. Consider the attribute *price* of food in a *restaurant*. As mentioned earlier in the book, a restaurant may have more than one range of prices; lunches may differ in price from diners, yet both may be obtained for a charge that is higher than the one for late-night snacks. If the domain includes all the prices charged by a restaurant, a sequence rule might help to keep data recording consistent. For example, "If a restaurant has more than one range of prices, record these price ranges according to the meal to which they apply, starting with breakfast."

Alternately, if values for an attribute are relatively long strings of symbols, a database designer may suggest—by formulating a *shortcut* rule—that some of the values be abbreviated, hopefully with no loss of information. The *frequency* of a *bus route* is an example here. Frequencies of buses can be expressed in various ways, and some ways are more economical than others. Aiming at efficient representation of data, a database designer may devise the following shortcut rule: "Record the frequency of a bus in one sentence if possible; e.g., every 10 minutes starting on the hour. Otherwise, list departure times from starting point."

The *quality* rule is another example of a rule governing for an irregularity that can be controlled. It may happen that the information taken from the authorized source of information "does not look right," or it does not have an expected quality. For example, the name of a restaurant does not seem like any other names, or the price charged seems imaginary. To guide a perplexed data collector, a database designer may formulate a *quality* rule. For the attribute *common name* of *location*, for instance, she instructs: "Record a common name of location even if it does not have the quality of a name; expressions such as 'where a bus ride is free,' or 'the biggest shopping mall in the Northwest' are acceptable common names."

All the domain rules described here are in the form of a general rule that elaborates on the definition of the domain. Some attributes, however, may require that their domains be explicitly listed. Such lists are called *authority lists*—they include all the valid values of an attribute. A simple example of an authority list is a list of ranges of prices that is the domain of *price* of *type of food*: C = less than $3, M = $3 to $6, E = $6 to $10, 0 = over $10.

While it is up to the discretion of a database designer to decide whether, for instance, *price* of *type of food* should be represented with codes from an authority list or whether it should follow a general rule, some attributes require the construction of authority lists from which their values are drawn.

Consider the attribute *name* of *type of food*. When we build the city database, we collect names of types of food from restaurant owners to compile a list of types of food. Such a list, however, requires some control on our part because some owners will claim, for instance, to serve Middle Eastern food while others call the same food type Árabic food. In the list, therefore, we would like to represent this type of food only once, and we can do so by exercising control and selecting only one name. The best way to facilitate a consistent recording of data is to provide an authority list of names of types of food. This list is then used when values for the attribute are collected.

Such a list has an additional advantage: It provides an hierarchical arrangement of types of food, which could also be used as an aid in determining the type of food that is served in a restaurant. Consider a restaurant that serves a few dishes from Brazil, Mexico, Cuba, and Argentina. A data collector can use the hierarchy in the authority list and characterize all these dishes as "Latin American." This would enable him to identify and to represent the major type of food served in the restaurant.

A more obvious example of an authority list would have been provided if the city database included the attribute *service,* which represents the issues that are the responsibility of each agency within the city administration. The domain of this attribute would be a list of all the subject matters that are addressed by the city's services, such as housing, food, and employment. A list of this kind resembles a list of subject descriptors, or subject headings, that are used for the retrieval of bibliographic information. An authority list of subject descriptors that is used for indexing and retrieval of information, in turn, is commonly called a thesaurus. The creation of an authority list for city services would, therefore, be guided by principles of thesaurus construction.

Fuzzy Domains

Rules for fuzzy domains are required when the data taken from the source of information do not correspond accurately to the domain and its characteristics, or when a domain includes values from other domains. The discrepancy between data found in the real world and the domain as defined by a database designer, or its values, manifests itself in a variety of instances. The following paragraphs describe several examples.

First, the data found in the source of information may not correspond to the definition of the domain. Restaurant licenses, for example, may include in their "address" area information that would not usually be considered address information—such as the number of the lot on which the restaurant is located or the number of the original building permit. While these elements of data were, in a way, sanctioned by city officials as relating to the address of a restaurant, a database designer could decide to eliminate these elements when the address of a restaurant is entered into the database. Thus, to resolve instances in which the data in a restaurant license do not correspond to the definition of the domain for *address*, a designer might formulate the rule: "Omit any information in the 'address' area of the license that is not part of the address."

Similarly, a rule must be created for instances in which the data from the source of information is incomplete. One may instruct, for example: "When the street number is not available, enter '0000'; when the street name is not available enter 'Street'; enter 99999 for unavailable zip codes."

Second, the values found in the source of information may not be valid values for the attribute. Consider the attribute *grade* of the relationship "graded." Suppose the source of information for the attribute is the actual review, and also that the domain is any alphanumeric string of symbols. This domain allows the grade to be recorded exactly the way it was coined by the reviewer, whether it is "very good," or "7 on a scale from 1 to 10." A cautious database designer, however, must anticipate other methods of expressing restaurant quality, even if they are not common. A designer may therefore, choose the rule: "When a grade is composed of characters that are neither numeric nor alphabetic, record it in words; e.g., three asterisks."

A similar example—and probably more obvious one—is the attribute *price* that is charged by a *restaurant*. As illustrated earlier, *price* can be expressed by two numbers separated by a hyphen, representing the range of prices that are charged. Here again, a cautious database designer would anticipate a situation in which a restaurant charges only one price for all its meals, such as "eat all you can" places. He would then decide whether the price such restaurants charge can be recorded as one number, or whether it should be recorded as a sequence of two identical numbers separated by a hyphen.

Third, the number of values found in the source of information may exceed the permitted limit. For example, even if a database designer limits the number of telephones a restaurant can have to one, some restaurants may have more than one telephone number. A rule that solves such a discrepancy is, "When an instance of a restaurant has more than one telephone number, record the first and add a ' + ' sign to designate that there are additional telephone numbers."

Fourth, two or more identical values may need to be distinguished. For example, it may happen that with a formula for creating restaurant codes, two restaurants are assigned the same code. While it may not bother us if two restaurants have the same name, the code for each restaurant should be unique because it is an identifier. Anticipating such a mishap, one would devise a rule, in addition to the general rule, that provides instructions about how to construct a code for a restaurant whose code has already been assigned to another restaurant.

Another example of this type of fuzzy domain, even though quite different, is the domain of the *frequency* of *bus route*. Most buses run on a given frequency during weekdays, but have a special schedule for weekends. Therefore, when recording the frequency of each bus in a database, it is necessary to designate the part of the week that is represented. Here, even if a certain special bus has a single frequency year-round, its frequency during weekdays should be distinguished from its frequency during weekends. Note that a rule to solve such discrepancies would be necessary whenever a divided attribute has only one set of values.

Fifth, the data taken from the authorized source of information might be questionable. In such cases a rule should instruct data collection personnel whether or not to adhere to the source and under what circumstances. "Record a restaurant address from the license even if you think it is incorrect" is an example of such a rule.

Last, special problems may arise when a domain includes values from other domains. An example of a rule to resolve that type of fuzzy domain is, "If the name of a restaurant is a name of a type of food, record it as the *name* of the *restaurant* only if it coincides with the type of food that is served in the restaurant." Note that this rule resolves more than one type of problem. While it instructs data collectors on how to deal with the cases in which the domain of the attribute *name* of *restaurant* includes a value from the domain *name* of *type of food*, it also solves the dilemma in which the "name" of a restaurant is questionable.

This example illustrates a pattern: While most rules are initially created to solve one type of problem, some are helpful in resolving other types as well.

DATA DICTIONARY ENTRIES

It is now time to examine again the entries for entities, relationships, and attributes in the data dictionary and to consider the additions that are required to facilitate a reliable data collection.

Data Dictionary Entries for Entities

A concept that is first introduced in this chapter is the *entity identifier*. Each entity calls upon a unique identifier whose purpose is to designate the representation of the entity in the database. At this point, we would also like to make a clear distinction between entries for entities and those for attributes. An easy way to facilitate this distinction is to add the letter "E" to the code of each entity.

Figure 7.4 illustrates the complete entries for entities in a data dictionary. The code for each entry begins with "E", and the attribute that serves as an identifier is recorded in a separate category. To provide for a smooth check of the completeness of the database, the attributes of each entity are listed in the entity's entry. Last, the rules are recorded in two sections corresponding to the rule types: Rules for Sources and Rules for Establishing Entities.

```
                         ENTITY

CODE E001                NAME Restaurant

DESCRIPTION A place where people who do not
            reside in it are served meals for
            a fee.

SOURCE D1           SYNONYM ___        SUBSET OF ___

IDENTIFIER Code

ATTRIBUTES Price, Name

RULES FOR SOURCES (a) The manager is the
preferred source of information.
(b) If the manager is also the owner, consult
the senior employee.
(c) If a restaurant has no manager, consult
the senior employee.

RULES FOR ESTABLISHING ENTITY (d) Any
establishment that satisfies the
description of a restaurant is a restaurant,
regardless of the number of employees, the
number of hours it provides services, the
number of diners, the method of payment,
or the variety of food it serves.
(e) If a restaurant has only one instance,
the restaurant is recorded both as a
restaurant and as an instance of a
restaurant.
```

```
                         ENTITY

CODE E003                NAME Type of food

DESCRIPTION The type of food a restaurant
            claims to serve.

SOURCE D3,D4,D13    SYNONYM __       SUBSET OF __

IDENTIFIER Name

ATTRIBUTES Price

RULES FOR SOURCES (a) The owner is the
preferred source of information.

RULES FOR ESTABLISHING ENTITY (b) The name of a
type of food should be clear, descriptive,
and self-explanatory.
```

Figure 7.4. Sample of completed entries for entities in the data dictionary

```
                              ENTITY

      CODE E012                NAME Location

      DESCRIPTION The actual place where an
                  establishment is located.

      SOURCE D14         SYNONYM E007        SUBSET OF ___

      RULES FOR SOURCES (a) The Official District
        Map of the City is the preferred source
        of information.

      RULES FOR ESTABLISHING ENTITY (b) A location
        must have a name that corresponds to a
        designated location in the Official District
        Map of the City.
        (c) If a shopping center houses more than
        twenty establishments it is considered a
        location; otherwise it is recorded as
        an address.
```

Figure 7.4. (Continued)

Data Dictionary Entries for Relationships

The data dictionary, as constructed from the Data Requirements Form and substantiated by the Operations Requirements Form, includes entries for items of data. When the Entity-Relationship Diagram was developed, these items of data were defined either as entities or as attributes. Relationships are recorded in the data dictionary only with the creation of the global schema; and as for entities and attributes, the information about each relationship is recorded on a separate card, or entry.

Relationships are different from entities and attributes because they do not represent objects but rather associations among these objects that are relevant to a database. The information stored in the data dictionary about relationships is, therefore, slightly different from the data recorded for entities and attributes (Figure 7.5).

To separate relationships from entities or from attributes, the code for each relationship starts with the letter "R." In addition,

```
                        RELATIONSHIP

CODE R001a   NAME Serves       CARDINALITY N:M
                               OCCURRENCE M (*)

CODE R001b   NAME Is served    CARDINALITY N:M
                               OCCURRENCE O (*)

ENTITY TYPES Restaurant, Type of food

ATTRIBUTES _____

RULES FOR SOURCES (a) The menu is the preferred
   source of information.
   (b) If a restaurant has no menu, accept
   information from the following sources,
   arranged in order of preference:
   (1) waiters, (2) chef, (3) manager, (4)
   owner, (5) diners.
   (c) If a restaurant has more than one menu,
   consult the menu printed most recently; and
   if all menus were printed at the same time,
   consult the one that includes the largest
   number of dishes.

RULES FOR ESTABLISHING RELATIONSHIP (d) The type
   of food that a restaurant serves is
   determined by the following procedure: each
   dish on the menu is assigned a type of food;
   the types of food are then ranked by number
   of dishes, eliminating types for which less
   than four dishes are available. The first
   three on the list are selected as types
   of food for the restaurant.
   (e) A restaurant can serve a type of food
   only if the type is listed in the Thesaurus
   of Types of Food.
   (f) A restaurant can serve up to three
   distinct types of food.
   (g) If there is no evidence that a restaurant
   serves a specific type of food, assign
   ''general'' as its type of food.
   (h) In case of doubt whether a restaurant
   serves a particular type of food, assign
   this type of food to the restaurant.
```

Figure 7.5. Sample of entries for relationships in the data dictionary

(i) Even if it is known that some dishes of a certain type of food are not actually served, select it as a type of food if it scores high enough using the procedure described in (d).

(j) If a restaurant has acquired a reputation for a particular type of food, assign this type to the restaurant even if it did not score high enough.

(*) M = mandatory; O = optional

RELATIONSHIP

CODE R002a   NAME Operates by   CARDINALITY 1:1
                               OCCURRENCE M (*)

CODE R002b   NAME Operates   CARDINALITY 1:1
                               OCCURRENCE M (*)

ENTITY TYPES Restaurant, License

ATTRIBUTES _____

RULES FOR SOURCES (a) The license itself is the preferred source of information.

RULES FOR ESTABLISHING RELATIONSHIP (b) A restaurant can be operated by a license only if the license has a number and an expiration date.

(c) If the license of a restaurant cannot be found, assign ''-0-'' as its number and ''none'' as its date.

(d) If it is not clear whether or not a license of a restaurant is valid, follow the instructions in (c).

(e) Even if you know that a license is about to be suspended, treat it as a valid license.

(f) If a restaurant has more than one license, record the earliest one.

(*) M = mandatory; O = optional

Figure 7.5. (Continued)

each relationship also has two sequential codes to represent each one of its directions. Next, the name of the relationship in each direction is recorded, followed by the occurrence—whether mandatory or optional—and by the cardinality of the relationship—whether 1:1, 1:M, or M:N.

The next category in the data dictionary entry for a relationship is the Entity Types that it associates. As you recall, relationships may also have attributes, such as the *date* on which a *restaurant* was "reviewed." Therefore, attributes are also recorded as well as both rules for sources and rules to establish relationships.

Once entries for relationships are established, the data dictionary can serve as the principal source of information about the data stored in a database, with the Entity-Relationship Diagram as a guide and as a means to obtain a general view of the database.

Data Dictionary Entries for Attributes

With the completion of the set of rules to be used for each attribute, the entries for attributes in the data dictionary can be updated to their complete format.

To distinguish between attributes and entities or relationships, the codes of attributes can be preceeded by the letter "A." While the Name, Description, Source, Synonym, and the Subset-of categories remain unchanged, a number of categories are added.

As illustrated in Figure 7.6, the next category is the Domain. Here we record the definition of the domain of each attribute. This definition may range from the most flexible definition, such as "any string of characters," to a rigorous requirement, such as "one letter." An efficient way to represent definitions of domains that have a predefined format is to use a notation that expresses the form of the valid values. The notation "L" can stand for the expression "one letter." Similarly, "N-N" represents the definition "two numbers separated by a hyphen," and "IIIIIII" indicates that the valid values for the attribute are strings of seven integers.

The next category to be added to the entry of an attribute is Entity/Relationship. In this category, we record the entity or the relationship to which the attribute belongs. Note that this category is crucial for attributes whose names recur, such as *name* or

```
                        ATTRIBUTE

CODE A004            NAME Telephone number

DESCRIPTION The number to call for information
            and reservations.


SOURCE D4          SYNONYM ___        SUBSET OF ___

DOMAIN III-III-IIII

ENTITY/RELATIONSHIP Instance of restaurant

CARDINALITY 1:1          OCCURRENCE O (*)

RULES FOR SOURCES (a) The Telephone Directory
   is the preferred source of information.
   (b) If there is no entry for a restaurant
   in the Telephone Directory, accept the
   following sources, arranged in order of
   preference: (1) an advertisement in a
   newspaper, (2) business card, (3) manager,
   (4) owner.

RULES FOR THE DOMAIN (c) A telephone number
   should be recorded as it appears in the
   authorized source.
   (d) Translate any letter that appears in the
   number as recorded in the source into an
   integer.
   (e) If an instance of a restaurant has
   more than one telephone number, record one
   and add a ''+'' sign to designate that
   there are additional telephone numbers.

RULES FOR ESTABLISHING ATTRIBUTE (f) If the
   number recorded in the source of information
   seems incorrect, do not assign it.
   (g) If an instance of a restaurant has more
   than one telephone number, record the one
   that is listed first.
   ----------------------

(*) M = mandatory; O = optional
```

Figure 7.6. Sample of completed entries for attributes in the data dictionary

```
                    ATTRIBUTE
     CODE A007          NAME Address

     DESCRIPTION What is written on a mailing label
                 when sending material to a certain
                 establishment.

     SOURCE D8        SYNONYM A012        SUBSET OF ___

     DOMAIN A string of characters

     ENTITY/RELATIONSHIP Instance of restaurant

     CARDINALITY 1:M        OCCURRENCE M (*)

     RULES FOR SOURCES (a) The restaurant's license
       is the preferred source of information.
       (b) If the license is unavailable, use any
       other reliable source.

     RULES FOR DOMAIN (c) Record the address exactly
       as it appears on the source of information.
       (d) If the address on the source does not
       include street number, street address, city,
       state, or zip code, acquire the missing
       information from any other reliable source.
       (e) If the street number is unavailable,
       enter ''0000''; if the name is unavailable,
       enter ''street''; enter 99999 for
       unavailable zip codes.
       (f) Omit any information in the source that
       is not part of the address.

     RULES FOR ESTABLISHING ATTRIBUTE (g) Record a
       restaurant address from the license even
       if you think it is incorrect.
     ----------------------
     (*) M = mandatory; O = optional
```

Figure 7.6. (Continued)

ATTRIBUTE

CODE A008   NAME Price

DESCRIPTION The average price that is charged
for providing commodities and
services.

SOURCE D9   SYNONYM ___   SUBSET OF A002

DOMAIN L

ENTITY/RELATIONSHIP Restaurant

CARDINALITY M:N   OCCURRENCE M (*)

RULES FOR SOURCES (a) The menu is the preferred
source of information.
(b) If a restaurant has no menu, accept
information from the following sources,
arranged in order of preference: (1)
waiters, (2) manager, (3) owner, (4) diners.
(c) If a restaurant has more than one menu,
consult the menu printed most recently. If
all menus were printed at the same time,
consult the one that includes the largest
number of dishes.

RULES FOR DOMAIN (d) If a restaurant has more
than one range of prices, record these in
ascending order, starting with the lowest
range.
(e) Record prices as follows: C = less than
$3, M = $3 to $6, E = $6 to $10, O = over $10.

RULES FOR ESTABLISHING ATTRIBUTE (f) Examine
the prices on the menu for dishes that are
neither appetizers nor desserts. The price
range starts with the second lowest price on
the list (unless there are at least three
dishes available in the lowest price), and
concludes with the highest price on the list
for which at least two dishes are available.
(g) If the price of food at a restaurant
cannot be determined using the designated
procedure, ask the manager to quote the
range of price.
(h) A restaurant can have no more than three
price ranges.

(*) M = mandatory; O = optional.

Figure 7.6. (Continued)

code. Following this category, the occurrence and the cardinality of the attribute are recorded.

Finally, the rules section of the entry is divided into three categories: Rules for Sources, Rules for Domain, and Rules for Establishing Attributes.

SUMMARY

Preparation for data collection includes the definition of entity identifier and attributes' domains, as well as the selection of rules. These decisions, which are part of the conceptual schema, are made on a general level to guide data collection in a later stage of database design.

An *entity identifier* is the string of symbols that represents an entity in a database. It should be unique to the entity it represents and easy to construct and decipher.

Similarly, a *value* of an attribute is the string of symbols that represents an attribute of a particular entity. The set of all the valid values of an attribute defines the *domain* of that attribute.

The purpose of the rules is to make the representation of objects and facts complete and unambiguous; they are formulated to counteract anticipated problems. There are two sets of rules that are pertinent to both entities and relationships, as well as to attributes: rules that determine authorized sources of information, and rules for establishing entities, relationships, and attributes. In addition, relationships and attributes require rules to define their occurrence and cardinality, and attributes require rules for the establishment of their domains.

Rules that determine authorized sources of information usually provide general instructions about which sources to use to gather information about entities, relationships, or attributes. Such a rule might specify a chief source, or it may allow the use of any available source. If only one source is selected, additional rules should specify which source to use in cases in which the chief source is lacking, and in those in which there is more than one source.

Rules for establishing entities, relationships, and attributes fall into one of three categories, according to the anticipated problems they are designed to resolve: (1) when the description of an entity, relationship, or an attribute may require some elaboration; (2) when several objects or facts could qualify as entities, relationships, or attributes to varying degrees—the case of fuzzy entities, relationships, or attributes; and (3) when an object or a fact can be defined either as one entity or attribute, or another (the borderline case).

Elaboration rules provide clarification or they emphasize subtle points. They may also furnish useful consistency checks. At times, such rules may simply provide a checklist of objects and facts that are considered as entities or attributes.

Rules for fuzzy entities and attributes provide additional criteria for establishing entities or attributes when more than one object or fact qualifies as an entity or an attribute. When entities, relationships, or attributes cannot be established straightforwardly, these rules determine procedures to establish them. In addition, they put a limit on the number of objects and facts that can be connected through a relationship or an attribute; they instruct how to "establish" a relationship or an attribute when it cannot be established according to general procedures; they guide data collection personnel in case of doubt; and they determine whether or not to use information that is known to be incorrect.

Borderline rules determine whether the object or fact in question will be recorded as two distinct attributes or as one. In the latter case, the rules also determine under what conditions each of the entities or attributes should be preferred.

Rules that determine the occurrence of relationships or attributes state whether a relationship or an attribute is optional or mandatory. The occurrence of some relationships and attributes is inherent to the state of affairs but it can be determined for others.

The cardinality of relationships and attributes refers to the number of objects and facts that can be connected through a relationship or an attribute: one-to-one, one-to-many, and many-to-many. While the cardinality of some relationships and attributes is a given, it can be decided for others.

Rules for domains deal primarily with how to establish a domain. A basic rule provides the most general instructions about how to select values. Some attributes may require that this rule be supplemented with a content rule, one that states what information to include in the values for each attribute. Such a rule may list the elements of information to be included, or it may state a mandatory minimum.

In addition, rules for specific exceptions may be required: when one knows that a value exists but is unable to find it; when a number of values should be recorded in a sequence; when some values need to be abbreviated; when the information taken from the authorized source "does not look right"; and when a domain needs to be listed in an authority list.

Rules for fuzzy domains are required when the data taken from the source of information do not correspond accurately to the domain and its characteristics, or when a domain includes values from other domains. Such rules resolve the following problems: the source provides an excess of information or incomplete information; it provides invalid values, or too many values; identical values need to be distinguished; the data available is questionable; and a domain includes values from other domains.

An entity identifier, as well as the occurrence and cardinality of relationships and attributes, is included in the Entity-Relationship Diagram. In addition, entries for relationships are established in the data dictionary; and entries for entities, relationships, and attributes are updated to include the additional information and the rules.

REFERENCE

1. Gorman, M. and Winkler, P. W. Ed. 1978. *Anglo-American Cataloging Rules.* *2nd ed.*, Chicago: American Library Association.

8

EVALUATION

The evaluation of the conceptual schema requires the testing of two types of features:

Rigorous Design Features. *These are critical for the database to be operative, and requirements placed by them should be fulfilled by the conceptual schema. Consistency, by which the definition of each component is consistent with definitions of other components, is an example of such a feature.*

Quality Features. *These affect the quality of the database, and requirements raised by them should be fulfilled as much as possible. Flexibility, by which conceptual schema accommodate changes in the represented world, and clarity, by which definitions and rules are made clear, are examples of such features. Quality features interact with one another: increasing flexibility may decrease clarity. Such trade-offs must be explicitly delineated so designers can assess the effect of their decisions on the quality of the conceptual schema.*

To evaluate the conceptual schema is to determine the "quality" of the database. The quality of a database, in turn, is determined by how well the database performs the functions it was designed to perform. It would seem, therefore, that the ultimate evaluation of a database can be carried out only when the database is in full operation. This conclusion is inaccurate for a number of reasons.

First, the concept of "ultimate evaluation" is not applicable to the dynamic world of databases; the environments and enterprise of a database are constantly changing, and the degree to which a database performs its functions fluctuates with such changes. Therefore databases need to be evaluated periodically, and they never reach a point where no further evaluation is necessary. In addition, there is no one measure that can be used to evaluate the performance of a database. In that sense, evaluation is not absolute; at best, it points out errors and exposes the weaknesses and strengths of a database. As we shall see in this chapter, trade-offs often exist among the various features of a database so that the improvement of one feature may weaken others.

Second, developing a database is a costly and time-consuming process. It is not realistic, therefore, to develop a database to its full-scale operation, only to learn about deficiencies in its design or possibly a failure in operation. Instead, every step in the design should be evaluated before the next one is taken. This reduces the probability of discovering unexpected deficiencies later on, when the database is fully developed.

This chapter presents the features of a database that should be evaluated throughout the design process. These features are of two kinds: those that are *necessary* for the design to be rigorous, and those *quality* features that improve the performance of the database. Necessary features are critical for the database to be operative, and quality features are critical for the database to be useful to its users. Features necessary for rigorous design include, for instance, the requirement that each entity type be clearly distinguished from other entity types, or that definitions of each component be consistent with definitions of other components. Requirements placed by these features should be satisfied by the conceptual schema. Alternately, quality features include characteristics such as the degree to which all the components that are needed for retrieval are included in the conceptual schema, or the degree to which the definitions and rules are clear. Requirements placed by these features should be satisfied by the conceptual schema as much as possible.

The chapter concludes with a discussion of the trade-offs that exist among quality features and with an evaluation of the data dictionary.

Most features presented in this chapter have been already discussed in previous chapters, at times at some length. This repetition is unavoidable because, to create a conceptual schema that is rigorously defined and useful, a design procedure must be used that is guided by these features. The method of building a conceptual schema presented in this book adheres to this principle. Therefore, using this method guarantees a consideration of most features throughout the design process. It is important, though, to discuss each individual feature so that a database designer can systematically evaluate the schema at each point of its development.

In addition, it is good practice to ask qualified personnel who did not participate in the development of a database to evaluate its design. Because they are uninformed about the deliberations and conflicts encountered throughout the design, such evaluators bring the fresh and unbiased view that is necessary for an unambiguous evaluation. While this book does not touch on the procedure for an outside evaluation, the features discussed here serve as a checklist to consider in such undertakings.

RIGOROUS DESIGN

A rigorous approach is necessary at every stage of the database design for a database to be operative. A systematic procedure for the design of the conceptual schema, and in particular the one presented here, facilitates rigorous design and is also necessary for this purpose. One should not assume, however, that using such a procedure automatically results in a design that is rigorous enough; a designer should check and re-check for slips, mistakes, or inconsistencies before the conceptual schema is completed.

Intrinsicality

The basic components of the conceptual schema are entities, relationships, and attributes. During the course of schema development, individual components are created, modified, shifted, or deleted. In principle, each decision relating to a component should be guided by the functions that a database is supposed to perform. By getting entangled with technical and logical issues, however, designers may overlook the relevance of the database requirements to a specific decision. As a result, the conceptual schema may include components that are not really necessary.

The *intrinsicality* of the conceptual schema requires that each entity type, relationship type, and attribute type relate to some function of the database. A conceptual schema is not rigorous if it includes components that do not contribute to the functions that the database is supposed to perform.

The home *address* of the *owner* of a restaurant, for example, might be included in a schema because a designer figured that it would be easy to obtain. Under such circumstances, entities that have an address should have that recorded as an attribute. Yet, the home address of a restaurant owner might be completely immaterial and of interest only to city officials (and they use the restaurant's address to correspond with the owner). In other words, no function that the database is supposed to perform requires this attribute. Intrinsicality requires that the attribute be eliminated.

On the practical level, the question is how to test whether a requirement raised by this feature is satisfied. Here, the operations dictionary (see Chapter 4), which stores data about the operations that cumulatively constitute the functions of the database, is an essential aid. In fact, one of the goals of the operations dictionary is to secure the intrinsicality of the design. It was used, you may recall, to guide the creation of the Entity-Relationship Diagram: The entities and attributes that were relevant to each operation were associated by establishing the proper relationships to create a mini-diagram, a building block of the general diagram. In other words, this dictionary is the principal source for the components that were included in the conceptual schema, and it guarantees that these components are actually *derived* from the functions the database is supposed to perform.

Before the conceptual schema is completed, however, it is necessary to check again whether all the components in it relate to the database's functions. A systematic procedure for this purpose is to check each entity, relationship, and attribute against the operations dictionary to ascertain that each can be related to at least one operation. One should bear in mind, however, that the operations dictionary is not error-free: Some operations might have been picked up later in the design and not added to the original dictionary. Therefore, the deletion of components that are not related to an operation should be performed cautiously, making sure that indeed no operation exists to which they are relevant.

Reliability

The *reliability* feature requires that for each entity type, relationship type, and attribute type there is information available in the real world and on the right level of specificity. This means that for each component in the conceptual schema—whether an entity, a relationship, or an attribute—the information available to the data collector is specific enough to establish the component, to apply the relevant rules, and to determine the value of each individual attribute. This requirement is important for rigorous design because database components are useless if the information that is necessary for their establishment does not exist.

It is important to note that reliability is a requirement for entity *types*, rather than for *individual* entities. Database designers should allow for the storage of incomplete or uncertain information about some individual entities, but they should not create an entity type when no reliable information to establish its members is available. The same maxim holds for relationships or attributes. Thus designers may establish the attribute *name* of a *reviewer* and conform with the reliability requirement because such names are usually readily available. Designers should, however, devise a rule that deals with the few exceptions in which the real name of a reviewer is unknown.

Reliability is a major force in formulating rules for entities, relationships, and attributes—rules that counteract problems in data collection. Nevertheless, even if such rules have been already formulated, it is important to check each component for this feature before the conceptual schema is completed.

An example can illustrate the importance of this requirement. Suppose a designer has selected the attribute *spiciness* to characterize each *type of food*. While the description of this attribute can be rather simple—the degree to which a food is spicy—some rules are necessary to explain how to establish the spiciness of a certain food, and how to actually express it. Suppose the designer aimed at accuracy and decided that the spiciness of food should be determined by applying the TANG test, which is a chemical procedure that provides a numeric grade to express the degree to which a food sample is spicy.

While such a rigorous rule is attractive, any evaluator of the conceptual schema should examine whether or not information about spiciness exists in the real world and if so, if it is specific enough. An evaluator is likely to find out that restaurants do not test their food for spiciness, and that at best they may indicate whether their food is hot, medium, or mild. In other words, no information is available about the TANG grades, and the information about the spiciness of food is not specific enough for the domain required for data collection. Now is the time to reconsider the definition of the attribute, its domain, and the rules for its establishment.

The designer may claim, for instance, that only the TANG test can reliably determine how spicy a food sample is because spiciness is usually a subjective measure—food that is spicy–hot to one person may be considered mild by another. However, in compliance with the requirement put forth by reliability, this accurate definition of the domain requires a modification. If the designer considers this attribute to be essential, he may decide to change the procedure for its establishment and its domain to require, say, that the spiciness of a type of food be determined by a short survey of a couple of restaurant owners who claim to serve that type of food. Alternately, the designer may decide to eliminate the attribute altogether because the information about it is not reliable enough.

The constraints dictionary (see Chapter 4), which organizes and controls the constraints on the data to be stored in a database, is a useful aid for determining the reliability of the conceptual schema. Each entry in the dictionary represents a constraint and the entities or attributes that are involved. While the dictionary is not likely to cover all instances in which information is not reliable, it points out entities and attributes that may present problems in this area.

Representability

While examining the previous features may result in the deletion of a component from the conceptual schema, this feature examines whether the conceptual schema indeed represents the real world. *Representability* requires that each individual entity, relationship, and attribute can be identified, and that the value for each attribute of an individual entity—in particular, its identifier—can be determined.

Put informally, for the conceptual schema to truly represent the real world, each object or fact and its associations that are relevant to a database must be easily identified and represented within the framework of the conceptual schema. Representability is the opposite of reliability. For a reliable schema, each component must be defined in a manner that agrees with the information available in the real world. In contrast, representability requires that each relevant piece of available information is represented in the database.

To check representability, evaluators could examine a sample of questions that data collectors encounter and test the ability of the guidelines provided by the conceptual schema to answer the questions. Such a test would determine the representability of a database: To satisfy the requirement placed by this feature, all the questions should be answered unambiguously. The sample could consist of these questions:

Nina Kitchen has just published a review about the Ham & Egg; should she be included in the database (i.e., is she a *reviewer*)?

Mr. Cook, a notable reviewer, was interviewed on his way out of The Ritz Cafe and his comments about the restaurant were aired on the late-night news; was the restaurant actually reviewed (i.e., does the relationship "reviewed" exist between the entities Mr. Cook and The Ritz Cafe)?

If Mr. Cook indeed reviewed The Ritz Cafe on this occasion, did he provide a grade (i.e., should the relationship "graded" and the attribute *grade* be established for this occasion)?

If Mr. Cook said The Ritz was an excellent place, which value should represent such a grade?

Scanning these questions, it is easy to see that they should be answered by rules for establishing entities, relationships, attributes, and domains. Therefore, representability requires that each component in the conceptual schema has a set of well-defined and unambiguous rules for its establishment. This requirement is most essential for relationships and domains because their entries in the data dictionary do not include a description. Thus, while some entities or attributes may not need a rule for their establishment—such as the *name* of a *restaurant*—because their description defines them well enough, each relationship and domain should have at least one rule for its establishment. In particular, it is important to verify that all the rules necessary for fuzzy entities, relationships, attributes, and fuzzy domain have been formulated, as discussed in Chapter 7.

Continuance

An additional issue that should be considered in the evaluation of the conceptual schema is whether the domain of each attribute is likely to stay unchanged during the lifetime of a database, or is a domain by its nature bound to change over time. *Continuance* requires that all domains are likely to be stable over time.

Domain stability requires that the definition of a domain remain unchanged. This implies that the value assigned to each individual attribute is likely to stay the same over time. Domain, however, is a set of all valid values for an attribute type, it should be distinguished from the set of values that have been assigned to an attribute type. The domain of an attribute type may be stable, yet the set of values assigned may change constantly as new attributes are added and others are deleted. Consider the attribute *name* of a *restaurant*. Its domain—"any string of characters"—is stable since it accommodates any kind of name and the name of each restaurant is likely to remain unchanged. On the other hand, the values assigned to this attribute in a database are likely to change constantly when new restaurants are established and others are closed down.

The continuance requirement is particularly important for attributes that serve as identifiers of entities. Consider, for instance, the entity *location* with its identifier, *name*. Suppose the name of a location is its official name, and the domain is the Official List of Districts. This is a valid domain for a city in which zoning is not likely to see any radical changes. On the other hand, if a city is growing rapidly and as a matter of course issues a new zoning scheme every two years, the Official List of Districts is bound to change with it. Here, the domain of the entity identifier is scheduled to change periodically, and with it the entity itself.

Thus the University District may cease to exist; part of its area could be annexed to the Freeway District and the rest included in a newly created district, the Union District. Such a change would result in a change in the definition of one entity (the Freeway District), an elimination of another entity (the University District), and the creation of yet a new entity (the Union District), which overlaps old entities. In addition, the relationships associated with this entity type should be modified for each individual entity: the location of each restaurant requires modification and so do bus routes going to each location.

If the domain of an identifier is bound to change constantly over time, the definitions of the individual entities are unstable and the entities are, therefore, not well defined over time. In the above example, a designer must establish a different identifier for *location*: an identifier with a stable domain, such as a map of the city that is divided arbitrarily into districts with the division kept unchanged. Clearly, this solution would usually be undesirable because this arbitrary division is artificial: It would be foreign to both users and data collectors. Under the circumstances, however, it might be the only solution available.

A word of caution is in order. One must not view continuance in an absolute sense. Databases are constructed to serve a dynamic world. It is expected that components will need modifications and some domains will change during the lifetime of a database. The domain of the *number* of a restaurant's *license*, for example, may be changed in the future from six to eight numbers. Yet, the license number is still the best identifier because it satisfies all the identifier's requirements and the definition of its domain is not *bound* to change constantly. In examining this feature, therefore, evaluators should clearly distinguish between domains that might see some changes and those that will inevitably go through many changes.

Resolution

The previous features required that the components defined in the conceptual schema be checked against reality. Rigorous design, however, puts forth some requirements for the internal structure of a schema as well. *Resolution* requires that each component in the conceptual schema be clearly distinguished from other components.

While each entity, relationship, and attribute should be checked for resolution, some components are more likely to generate problems in resolution. In the example of the schema for the function "Going to a restaurant," an evaluator should test—preferably with the aid of real examples—if the attribute *address* can be always clearly distinguished from the entity *location*. The entities *restaurant* and *instance of restaurant* require scrutiny as well, and so do the relationships "reviewed" and "graded." As with other features, these issues are not new: We discussed them earlier when we defined these components. A check for resolution, however, should be performed after all the components have been defined and before the conceptual schema is completed.

Consistency

Another requirement for rigorous internal structure is the demand for internal consistency. Internal *consistency* requires that the definition of each component be consistent with definitions of other components.

A database designer is not likely to overlook the requirement for consistency among components that relate directly to one another. Thus the definition of the entity *license* must be consistent with the definition of *restaurant*, so that a license that is granted by the city is related to the establishment that received it. Similarly, the rules for establishing the relationship "reviewed" should be consistent with those for the establishment of the relationship "graded": One may need to state explicitly whether a restaurant can be graded if it has not been reviewed, and whether a restaurant is graded *whenever* it is reviewed.

The need for checking consistency among components that are not directly related, on the other hand, is not always obvious. In theory an evaluator should check each pair of components for consistency. One should bear in mind, however, that the method of conflict resolution by which the global schema has been constructed (see Chapter 6) guarantees that the definitions of the components in the conceptual schema are consistent with one another. During its application, each component is checked against the other components in the temporary global schema to resolve conflicts that cause inconsistency.

Nevertheless, an evaluator could apply some general checks for consistency, such as the requirement that domains of attributes with the same name be consistent with one another. Thus he might require that the attribute *address*, for example, has the same domain whether it is an address of a restaurant, a reviewer, or a city department. While it makes sense to require that domains of all instances of the attribute *address* be of the same form, such a general requirement does not always apply. The name of a restaurant, for instance, has a form that is different from that of a name of a person—whether a reviewer, an owner, or a fire marshal. Therefore, while names of persons should have the same form across a database, that form should not be compared with the one used for restaurants.

Like other features, consistency should be examined rigorously but not mechanically, allowing for the flexibility required for a database to interact with the real world.

QUALITY FEATURES

Features of rigorous design are necessary for a database to be operative; quality features, on the other hand, place requirements for the improvement of a database. These features are extremely important: If they are neglected, a database might be operative but useless. They designate quality rather than necessity because it is impossible to achieve maximum compliance with all their requirements in a single database. As we see in the section "Trade-offs," the requirements are interrelated and are often contradictory with one another.

Flexibility

One of the important characteristics of a database is its ability to remain useful over a period of time, during which period the world is likely to experience changes. *Flexibility* assesses the degree to which the conceptual schema can accommodate changes in the real world it represents.

To check the flexibility of a database, an evaluator could test how well the conceptual schema accommodate hypothetical changes that may occur in the future. For each such hypothetical situation, the evaluator checks the success of the database in providing information related to the issue at hand, and what modifications in the conceptual schema are required, if any. If, for example, a component is missing from the schema, could it be added? If it is added, how would it affect the conceptual schema?

An evaluator may consider, for instance, the day when bus drivers are on strike. Here, one question to ask is whether users would be able to retrieve information about how to get to a restaurant. This question has several aspects. First, are there components in the schema that facilitate the provision of information about other means of transportation? Examining the Entity-Relationship Diagram we have constructed for the function "Going to a restaurant" (see Figure 7.3), we see the answer is "no."

Second, the evaluator needs to decide if he thinks subways and taxis should be added to the conceptual schema and, if so, whether to suggest that such additions be made right away, or be postponed until the need for such information arises. No matter what the recommendation is, the evaluator should examine whether or not these new components can be added to the conceptual schema. Checking our example, one can easily see that there is no reason why these components could not be added.

Third, the evaluator must consider the impact of such additions on the conceptual schema. In the example, it seems that the entity type *subway* can be easily added to the Entity-Relationship Diagram and be presented in a manner similar to the representation of the entity type *bus route*. Adding *taxi*, however, is not as straightforward. As shown in Figure 7.3, *bus route* is related to *location* so that each route is associated with the locations that it "goes to." Taxis, on the other hand, can go to any location. Therefore, they cannot be associated with *location* in the same manner buses are. Yet taxis are important for the database because they can go to locations. Clearly, a different kind of relationship is needed between *taxi* and *location*. Now is the time for the database designer to step in and reconsider the representation of the various means of transportation.

While the previous example illustrated a case in which new entity types are required, changes in the real world over time may also affect domains. Consider, for example, the introduction of a new type of food: East African. The relevant questions here are, Could it be added to the authority list of types of food, and how would it affect the list and the schema? Other hypothetical types of food could be proposed and the ability of the list and the schema to accommodate them tested.

A check for flexibility may sometimes require that the evaluator reconsider the definition of a component. Consider, for example, the entity type *restaurant* and its description: "A place where people who do not reside in it are served meals for a fee." Suppose that a new "eating place" becomes fashionable—the Keep Trim restaurant. In it people are served hypnotic meals: While no real food is served, people leave the restaurant believing they just had a satisfying meal. Because it is a popular restaurant, we would like to have information about Keep Trim in the database.

Here an evaluator needs to ask, Is the definition of a restaurant flexible enough to include that kind of restaurant? One may argue that only a clarification is needed to explain that meals can be real or imaginary. Another evaluator or designer, on the other hand, may claim that such an interpretation contradicts commonsense. Suppose, though, that a modification is agreed on (after all, if hypnotic meals are actually available, meals can indeed be imaginary). How would such a modification affect the other entities and attributes that are associated with *restaurant*? The entity *chef* (not shown in Figure 7.3), for example, would need to accommodate for "chefs" of hypnotic meals, and so would *type of food*. In short, the definitions of all the components associated with *restaurant* must be reconsidered in light of the new interpretation of the concept of meal.

The requirement that the conceptual schema be flexible must be kept in mind throughout the design process. While a final examination of this feature should be carried out when the conceptual schema is completed, checking for flexibility should not be postponed to the last moment because it may result in major reconsiderations that are not desirable at such a late stage.

Clarity

Definitions of components and their rules must be clear for the data collection personnel and for users retrieving information. Therefore, *clarity*, which designates the degree to which definitions and rules can be applied in an unambiguous and understandable way, is also an important feature of the schema.

Clarity is related to representability, which is a feature of rigorous design: To provide for the requirement that each object or fact in the real world be easily identified, it is desirable to formulate clear definitions and rules. Clarity, however, requires that definitions and rules be formulated so that their application is objective. Consider again East African food. A database that complies with representability would provide for an immediate recognition that East African is a type of food and that it is not included in the domain of the entity identifier. A database that conforms with clarity would, in addition, include clear instructions (so that all data collectors and users interpret them the same way) about whether to add this new food type or whether to ignore it.

While clarity is an important feature, at times it might be preferable to keep a definition somewhat open-ended or vague to facilitate other database requirements. Consider, for example, the attribute *special services* that are offered in a restaurant (not shown in Figure 7.3). As illustrated in Chapter 5 these services include events such as live music, valet parking, or birthdays for kids. In creating this attribute, a designer may consider two opposing options. The first, which conforms with clarity, is to establish a Special Services List that would include all such services, and to define the attribute in terms of the list: "All services provided by a restaurant that are included in the Special Services List." In this case, the definition of the attribute is clear and the domain is well defined; examining each service provided by a restaurant, a data collector can easily decide whether or not it is a special service.

This option, however, results in a conceptual schema that is not flexible. New special services are bound to emerge in this competitive world of restaurants, and services that are special at one time may become quite ordinary at a future time. The list, then, would soon become outdated, along with the definition of the attribute. The requirement for continuance (see previous section) prevents us from constantly changing the attribute's domain—the Special Services List. To enhance flexibility, therefore, a database designer must consider the second option: a definition for the attribute *special services* that is somewhat open-ended.

A slightly vague definition for this attribute is, "Any service that is not ordinarily provided." The domain in this case is open-ended—any string of characters—and data collectors are supposed to check each service provided by a restaurant and decide if it qualifies as a special service. The definition of this attribute is open-ended in the sense that it allows a data collector to use his own judgment and thus improve flexibility, while keeping within requirements for rigorous design.

Deviations from clarity should be made only to accommodate other quality or necessary features of the conceptual schema, and they should be limited to workable definitions and rules so that representability is not affected.

Efficiency

One of the basic considerations in the design of a conceptual schema is its efficiency. Many decisions discussed in previous chapters were guided by this feature. Ideally, one would like to have only the minimum number of components in the conceptual schema and still create a database that performs all the required functions, comply with all the requirements for rigorous design, and score highly on the quality features. Therefore, *efficiency* is defined as the number of entity types, relationship types, and attribute types with relation to the functions the database is supposed to perform.

One way to check for efficiency is to see that redundancy is limited to a necessary minimum—the principle of *minimum redundancy*. Suppose an evaluator discovers that both entities *restaurant* and *instance of restaurant* are related to the entity *owner*. An alert evaluator must check whether or not these relationships are redundant. Clearly, if an owner of a restaurant is always the owner of all its instances, the relationship between *owner* and *instance of restaurant* is redundant. On the other hand, large restaurant chains often franchise each instance of their restaurants to a different owner, in which case the redundancy is necessary.

It is difficult to formulate general guidelines for efficiency tests. One of the reasons for the difficulty is that it is not always clear what is efficient, or what would be lost for efficiency. Another reason is that efficiency can be improved in so many different ways that no single set of guidelines could address the large variety of means for efficiency enhancement.

On the other hand, the efficiency of the conceptual schema was one of the major features considered in building the Entity-Relationship Diagram, in integrating the local schemata, and in formulating rules for data collection (see Chapters 5 through 7). A few examples can illustrate the important role efficiency plays in these processes.

To increase efficiency, one can create an instance of an entity (see Chapter 5). In this way, attributes that are common to a number of individual entities are represented in one entity (the entity itself) and attributes that are likely to change from one individual entity to another are gathered in another entity (the instance of the entity). Thus repetition of common values is eliminated, even though the number of entity types is increased. Another example is the recommendation that no relationship be established between *restaurant* and *bus*, but rather that one be established between *bus* and *location*. Thus *restaurant, movie theater, museum,* or *concert hall* are not related individually to *bus* but to their *location*, which is then related to *bus*.

In addition, deciding whether an item of data should be designated as an entity or an attribute (see Chapter 5) is guided by efficiency considerations. Attributes are more efficient than entities: They do not require an identifier, and they are associated with an entity (or a relationship) with no explicit relationship. Therefore, the establishment of an attribute generates a smaller number of components than would be required for the establishment of an entity in the conceptual schema. Thus an item of data that could be defined as an attribute must not be established as an entity. Similarly, we introduced the concept of divided attributes (see Chapter 5) to avoid the creation of additional attributes when a single attribute can be divided.

Semantic Integrity

The establishment of entities, relationships, and attributes was guided by the operations dictionary: for each operation a mini-diagram of the components involved was constructed. Such a procedure for constructing the Entity-Relationship Diagram fosters a direct relationship among entities that need to be associated for a particular operation. Thus, because the operation "Select type of food" (Figure 4.2), for example, involves the data items *restaurant* and *type of food*, these items were established as two distinct entities associated by the relationship "serves."

Some operations, however, can be represented by components that already exist, even if the associations among them are not direct. The operation "Find price of type of food" (not listed in Figure 4.2), for example, can be satisfied by the existing diagram because the answer to the question about the price of a certain food type can be *inferred* from the existing components. *Semantic integrity* assesses the capability of a database to support the development of meaningful inferences.

Like other features of the conceptual schema, semantic integrity should be examined in the earlier stages of schema development. In fact, we used this requirement implicitly in the previous examples. To increase efficiency in design, we decided to associate *bus route* with the *location* of a *restaurant* rather than with the *restaurant* itself. However, so that a database user can find out which bus goes to a restaurant, we created a network of relationships with semantic integrity. A meaningful inference can be made to answer such questions.

Even if this feature has been considered throughout the development of the conceptual schema, it should be examined again by testing a set of hypothetical questions. Semantic integrity could be examined by testing how well the conceptual schema answers these questions: What types of food have been reviewed by Mr. Cook? What bus should Mr. Latif take to get to the Minaret restaurant? What types of food are served by high-quality restaurants (grading "good" and above) located in the University District?

To complement this somewhat intuitive test, an evaluator may check semantic integrity by ascertaining that each component of a conceptual schema is associated—directly or indirectly—with a focal entity—an entity that is central to an Entity-Relationship Diagram (see Chapter 5). Such a test by itself cannot guarantee semantic integrity because it does not check associations among focal entities. These associations, however, should not be checked because they are not necessary for semantic integrity: Some focal entities are not associated with others because no future question to the database will require these associations. While associations among nonfocal and focal entities are not the ultimate test for semantic integrity, they at least provide for a systematic procedure to examine a condition that is necessary.

Completeness

Every method for the construction of the conceptual schema must have some built-in procedures which check that everything that needs to be covered by the database is indeed included. *Completeness* estimates the degree to which all the entity types, relationship types, and attribute types that are needed for information retrieval are included in the conceptual schema.

Completeness is the opposite requirement to intrinsicality, which is necessary for rigorous design (see "Intrinsicality"). There we required that each component in the conceptual schema be related to some function of the database; here we examine whether each function of the database is represented in the conceptual schema, and with the relevant components. While intrinsicality is necessary, completeness is considered a quality feature because it could never be achieved in an absolute sense. No matter how thorough and systematic our design is, we can never guarantee that *all* future functions of the database have been considered in its analysis and design.

Another complication with this feature is that the "true" test of completeness is best conducted when the operation of the database is actually tested. In testing, the database is examined for its ability to answer a set of anticipated requests, or questions in a limited realm. Although it is difficult to evaluate a conceptual schema for its completeness, designers strive to fulfill this feature throughout the development of the schema.

Specificity

Most of the previous features examined the relationship between the real world and the conceptual schema, or they placed requirements on the structure of the conceptual schema. One should also examine, however, the ability of the database to provide potential users with answers that are meaningful to them. One aspect of this condition is the *specificity* of the conceptual schema, or the degree to which the database can answer questions on the level of specificity required.

Loosely put, this feature requires that entities, relationships, and attributes are not too broad to be useful. If each restaurant, for example, requires one license for its operation and another for alcoholic beverages, the entity *license* is too broad. Using it as one entity, a city official would have no way to determine the number of licenses given to the Minaret restaurant for its operation. Similarly, if all city personnel who are involved with a restaurant—

whether inspectors, specialists, or fire marshals—are represented by one entity, *person*, that is associated with *restaurant* in one relationship, "assigned to," there is no way to determine which inspector is assigned to the Minaret restaurant. The relationship "assigned to" is too broad (see Chapter 6, "Conflict between Definitions").

This feature relates directly to users and their information needs. The requirement for specificity is satisfied most easily when the design of the conceptual schema is guided by information needs, as illustrated in this book.

Domain Specificity

Like other components of the conceptual schema, domains of attributes should concur with the level of specificity required. The feature *domain specificity* judges the degree to which the valid values defined in a domain are specific enough.

The level of specificity for each domain is determined when the domain is established. At that time a designer matches the specificity of a domain with the specificity needed in information retrieval. Thus a designer is likely to decide that the *grade* given to a *restaurant* by a *reviewer* will not just be good or bad. Most people are more sophisticated in their requirements for information and they would like to know, say, how a restaurant would rank on a scale from 1 to 5. Therefore, the domain of this attribute should include at least five valid values. On the other hand, one may decide that information about bus *frequency* should not be as specific as it first seems. Rather than listing all times of departure and arrival to each bus stop, a less specific (but more efficient) schedule may be provided to users, one that lists the starting time and the time frequency, such as every 10 minutes. While the second option is less specific than the first one, it is still specific enough for the information retrieved to be meaningful.

Specificity, however, may take other forms. Consider, for example, the entity *type of food* and its identifier *name*. Suppose the domain of this attribute is an authority list of names of types of food. Specificity here is also determined by the degree of order within the list: The more organized the list is, the more specific is the domain. An example can illustrate this principle. Suppose the authority list is broken into categories—for simplicity's sake, assume the two categories spicy–hot and mild food. With such categories, the name of each type of food provides an additional characteristic of the food, whether spicy–hot or mild, depending on the category to which the food belongs.

Generally, the more information is given in a value of an attribute, the more specific the value is. Thus "McBurger on Greenlake" is more specific a name of a restaurant than just "McBurger," and the telephone number "206-543-1234" is more specific than "543-1234." For the information retrieved from the database to be meaningful, values of a domain should be as specific as *required* rather than as *possible*.

Domain Expressiveness

The *expressiveness* of a domain is a concept that designates the degree to which a domain allows for the expression of the various characteristics of an entity. This requirement is so fundamental that we have discussed it in many of the previous examples even though we did not mention its name.

We improved the expressiveness of domains when we decided, for example, to add the term "general" to the authority list for types of foods. This enables a data collector to designate the "type of food" that is served in restaurants that do not serve a particular type of food, and also allows a user to select a restaurant that does not specialize in a particular food type. On another occasion, we decided to allow for a number of price ranges to be assigned to one restaurant, so that the price for its light menu as well as the one for the more substantive menu could be recorded—a move that increases how well the attribute *price* expresses the various characteristics of a restaurant. Similarly, establishing an open-ended domain for the attribute *special services* increases its expressiveness, as does the definition of the domain of the *name* of a *restaurant* ("any string of characters").

Expressiveness concludes the list of necessary and quality features of the conceptual schema that are important for the design of a database. The following section illustrates how the quality features relate to one another.

TRADE-OFFS

One of the most important issues of database evaluation is the consideration of trade-offs. No database can perform best on *all* features; improving one feature is likely to cause a reduced performance in other features. A database cannot achieve *maximum* performance for all purposes because such a point does not exist. It is imperative that designers and evaluators of databases recognize this characteristic and develop a database that operates optimally under given conditions.

Examples of trade-offs are abundant in this book. We have just demonstrated that to increase *flexibility* we may need to reduce *clarity* and use an open-ended definition for the entity *special services*. Our decision to reduce *specificity* in recording the *frequency* of a *bus route* in order to increase *efficiency* is another example. *Completeness* and *efficiency* can also contradict one another: A designer may decide to establish *telephone number* as an undivided attribute so that only the reservations number is recorded in the database. While the conceptual schema is not complete because telephone numbers for the managers of restaurants are not recorded, it is efficient because it avoids unnecessary redundancy: When a restaurant has one telephone number, for both reservations and managers, this number is recorded only once in the database.

The last example illustrates two important principles. First, the decision about whether one feature of the database is more important than another should be determined by the conditions in which the database operates and by database specifications. The decision to keep the *telephone number* undivided is valid—even though the database is incomplete—when, say, most restaurants have only one telephone number anyway, or when it is unlikely that users will be interested in the manager's number. On the other hand, if the development of the database is supported by the city, and if city officials need to know the managers' numbers for their daily tasks, it would make sense to sacrifice efficiency for the sake of completeness, and to always include both numbers even if they are the same—a solution that introduces redundancy.

Second, faced with the need to introduce a modification to improve the performance of a database, a designer should select the route that has the least effect on the other features of the database. In other words, one should always attempt to improve one feature with minimum reduction in the ability of the database to comply with other features. A designer should, for instance, examine whether or not the contradiction between completeness and efficiency presented in the last example could be softened. Indeed, a compromise could be found. The attribute *telephone number* could be divided but in such a way that the manager's telephone number is recorded *only* if it is different from the reservations number. This way, while design is a little less efficient because the attribute is divided, unnecessary redundancy is eliminated and completeness is optimal.

Database designers and evaluators must be aware of the trade-offs involved in each decision they make. Not being able to clearly identify such relationships is a major obstacle to database design. Once trade-offs are explicitly defined, the decision about which design solution to select should be guided by database specifications and by the effect that each solution would have on other features.

DATA DICTIONARY

The data dictionary is a major part of the conceptual schema because it includes information about the data that are included in the database. It is, however, a database by itself. All the features that are important for the evaluation of a database are therefore applicable to the evaluation of the data dictionary.

The flexibility of the data dictionary determines whether it can accommodate future changes in its entries. If coding, for example, is not flexible enough, additions or deletions might present difficulties. Similarly, for the data dictionary to be complete, it should include entries for all the entities, relationships, and attributes. Another example is clarity that determines the degree to which the order and the arrangement of the entries can be understood unambiguously.

The data dictionary, however, is a special kind of database because it includes information about data. As such it is characteristically an authority list, or a thesaurus. Therefore, design considerations for a data dictionary should include considerations typical of the design for a thesaurus. It is beyond the scope of this book to discuss thesaurus construction, and the reader is advised to consult texts dedicated to this subject—e.g.,(see *Indexing Languages and Thesauri* [1]). Two important aspects—which usually are not that obvious—are mentioned here, however.

First, when entities and attributes are first recorded in the data dictionary, their general relationships with other entities and attributes—those relationships that are not specific to the database—are recorded (see Chapter 4). As shown in Figures 4.1, 7.4, and 7.6, the dictionary entries include the categories Synonym and Subset-of. The Synonym category represents entities and attributes that closely relate to the entry's entity or attribute. Thus, the attribute *address* is recorded as a synonym for the entity *location,* and *quality* is synonymous to *being fancy.* Similarly, *cleanliness* is a subset of *quality.*

It is important to identify and record these relationships because they facilitate resolution, consistency, and clarity checks. In addition, they can be utilized to help users in information retrieval. If a user, say, is not satisfied with the information she retrieves about the quality of a restaurant, she can be advised to search for information about the cleanliness of the restaurant, or to find out whether or not it is fancy. Important as they are, establishing such relationships is not inherent to the development of the conceptual schema. Database designers, therefore, may put this task aside, or worse yet, forget to accomplish it. It is the responsibility of an evaluator to see that these relationships among entities and attributes are identified and recorded in the data dictionary.

Second, access to entries in the data dictionary may depend on word usage. If a data collector, for example, wishes to find the rules for establishing the attribute *cleanliness* of a *restaurant*, she would look under the entry for this attribute by name. Suppose, though, that a database designer selected the term *health hazards* to express the cleanliness of a restaurant; our data collector would not be able to find the relevant entry unless she was directly referred to it.

One method of avoiding such mishaps is to construct a *lead-in vocabulary.* This vocabulary includes all the terms that could have been selected to designate entities or attributes but were rejected. Each term in this vocabulary leads to the "legitimate" name of the entity or the attribute. Thus a data dictionary would have an entry for *cleanliness,* but it would only designate that the term to use is *health hazards.*

A database designer has to construct a lead-in vocabulary for data dictionaries that provide names of entities and attributes as access points. An evaluator of such a data dictionary should check whether this vocabulary is complete and specific enough. Note that not only is the data dictionary a database and at the same time a thesaurus, it is a thesaurus of a special kind: It may include other thesauri. The data dictionary is a thesaurus of entity types, relationship types, and attribute types, and therefore it includes the definitions of domains. Domains, on the other hand, may themselves be thesauri, such as the list of food types or the list of official names for locations. Thus methods of thesaurus construction should be used both for data dictionaries and for the thesauri they contain.

SUMMARY

The evaluation of a database can be performed only when the database is operative. One can evaluate the conceptual schema, however, when it is completed and before data are collected. To evaluate the conceptual schema, an evaluator tests a host of features: To ensure rigorous design they check features that are critical for the database to be operative; and to ensure the quality of the design, they test quality features that are critical for the database to be useful. Requirements placed by features for rigorous design should be satisfied, while those placed by quality features should be satisfied as much as possible.

Six features of rigorous design can be identified:

Intrinsicality requires that each component of the conceptual schema relates to some function of the database

Reliability requires that for each component of the conceptual schema, there is information available in the real world and on the right level of specificity

Representability requires that each individual entity, relationship, or attribute can be identified, and that the value of each attribute of an individual entity can be determined

Continuance requires that all domains are likely to be stable over time

Resolution requires that each component of the conceptual schema be clearly distinguished from other components

Consistency requires that the definition of each component be consistent with definitions of other components

There are eight quality features:

Flexibility assesses the degree to which the conceptual schema can accommodate changes in the world it represents

Clarity designates the degree to which definitions and rules can be applied in an unambiguous and understandable way

Efficiency examines the number of schema components with relation to the functions the database is supposed to perform

Semantic integrity assesses the capability of a database to support the development of meaningful inferences

Completeness estimates the degree to which all the entity types, relationship types, and attribute types that are needed for information retrieval are included in the conceptual schema

Specificity is the degree to which the database can answer questions on the level of specificity required

Domain specificity judges the degree to which the valid values defined in a domain are specific enough

Domain expressiveness designates the degree to which a domain allows for expression of the various characteristics of an entity

Quality features interact among themselves and, therefore, a database cannot achieve maximum quality for all purposes at the same time. The trade-offs among these features, however, can be discovered and thus guide design decisions. A trade-off might exist, for instance, between flexibility and clarity: To provide for better flexibility, one may use an ambiguous definition for an entity. Recognizing this trade-off, a designer can base his design decision on the relative importance of each of the two features to a specific database.

The data dictionary is itself a database, and it should be evaluated by both the features for rigorous design and quality. In addition, the data dictionary is a thesaurus of schema components and its development should follow principles of thesaurus construction. In particular, designers must pay attention to establishing relationships among entity types and attribute types, and to the construction of the lead-in vocabulary.

REFERENCE

1. Soergel, D. 1974. *Indexing Languages and Thesauri: Construction and Maintenance.* Los Angeles, CA: Melville.

GLOSSARY

Attribute: A piece of information about an entity or about a relationship.

Cardinality of relationships: A rule that determines how many individual entities in an entity type can be associated with one entity in the other entity type, and vice versa: one-to-one, one-to-many, or many-to-many.

Clarity: A term that designates the degree to which definitions and rules could be applied in an unambiguous and understandable way.

Classification of sentences: The procedure for organizing the data recorded in the Requirements Collection forms by analyzing each sentence for the information it includes.

Completeness: This feature is a measure of the degree to which all the entity types, relationship types, and attribute types that are needed for information retrieval are included in the conceptual schema.

The conceptual schema: A diagramatic presentation, or a formal outline, that explicitly expresses all the decisions on the conceptual level. It includes the Entity-Relationship Diagram and the entries in the data dictionary with the relevant rules.

The conceptual level of design: The level that relates to the representation of the entire enterprise in a database.

Consistency: The requirement that the definition of each entity type, relationship type, and attribute type be consistent with definitions of other entity types, relationship types, and attribute types.

Constraints dictionary: A dictionary, or a database, that stores information about constraints that exist in the database's enterprise or in its environment.

Constraints form: The form used to record restrictions on the enterprise or on environments.

Continuance: The requirement that domains are likely to be stable over time.

Data administrator: See **Enterprise administrator.**

Data dictionary: A dictionary, or a database, that stores information about data that are relevant to a database.

The data model: See **Conceptual schema, The.**

Data requirements analysis: See **Requirements analysis.**

Data Requirements Form: The form used to collect data about the enterprise.

Database: A store of data about a selected part of the real world that is intended to be used for particular purposes.

Divided attribute: An attribute that has more than one component, for example, *high* and *low* price.

Domain: A set of values that could be assigned to represent an attribute; it forms the pool from which the valid values of an attribute can be drawn.

Domain expressiveness: This term designates the degree to which a domain allows for expressing the various characteristics of an entity.

Domain specificity: This requirement judges the degree to which the valid values defined in a domain are specific enough.

Efficiency: The requirement to examine the number of entity types, relationship types, and attribute types with relation to the functions that the database is supposed to perform.

Enterprise: The part of the real world about which data are stored in a database.

Enterprise administrator: A person who is primarily responsible for decisions on the conceptual level.

Entity: A "thing" that can be distinctly identified; any distinguishable object, real or abstract, that is to be represented in a database.

Entity identifier: A string of symbols that represents an object in a database.

Entity-Relationship Diagram: A graphical representation of the elements in a conceptual schema.

Entity type: A set of entities of the same type.

Environment: Information needs arising from a particular purpose that a database was constructed to fulfill.

Expressiveness: See **Domain expressiveness.**

The external level of design: The level that relates to the particular views of the data that are geared to specific purposes. Examples: a means to express a request, the interface language, a picture of the arrangement of the data, a picture of the possible manipulation of data, and formats for display of answers.

Flexibility: This characteristic is an assessment of the degree to which the conceptual schema can accommodate changes in the real world it represents.

Focal entity: An entity that is central to an Entity-Relationship Diagram, or to a part of the diagram.

Functional chart: A chart that represents the functions that are performed in an organization and their relationships to one another.

Global schema: A conceptual schema for a whole database.

Identifier: See **Entity identifier.**

Integrated database: A database that puts together a number of data stores into one data store, eliminating redundancy in the data stored.

The internal level of design: The level that relates to how the data are actually stored. Examples: the medium on which data are stored, the format in which data are stored, the methods used to provide access to data, the amount of information provided with each entry, and the internal organization of entries.

Intrinsicality: The requirement that each entity type, relationship type, and attribute type relate to some function of the database.

Local schema: A conceptual schema created for one function of a database.

The logical model: See **Conceptual schema, The.**

Occurrence Rule: A rule that states whether or not a relationship or an attribute is mandatory.

Operation: An activity or action taken by potential users to fulfill a function that a database is designed to support.

Operations dictionary: A dictionary, or a database, that stores data about the operations that cumulatively constitute the functions under consideration for a database.

Operations Requirements Form: The form used to record actions that users take to perform the functions that are analyzed.

Organizational chart: A chart that reflects the administrative structure of an organization.

Relationship: An association among entities.

Reliability: The requirement that for each entity type, relationship type, and attribute type there is information available in the real world and on the same level of specificity.

Representability: The requirement that each individual entity, relationship, or attribute can be identified, and that the value for each attribute of an individual entity—in particular, its identifier—can be determined.

Requirements analysis: The process of exploring potential information needs and future requirements that users will bring to a database.

Requirements collection: See **Requirements analysis.**

Requirements Collection Form: The form used to record raw data, as collected from interviews and/or observations of potential users.

Resolution: The requirement that each entity type, relationship type, or attribute type be clearly distinguished from other entity types, relationship types, and attribute types.

Semantic integrity: The feature that assesses the capability of a database to support the development of meaningful inferences.

Shared database: A database that has more than one environment.

Specificity: The degree to which the database can answer questions on the level of specificity required. See also **Domain specificity.**

Structured analysis: A method that uses techniques of systems analysis to analyze the functional structure of an organization.

Structured design: See **Structured analysis.**

Structured system analysis: See **Structured analysis.**

Temporary global schema: A conceptual schema that is the result of the integration of two or more local schemata. It is constantly growing as additional schemata are integrated into it to eventually establish the global schema.

Users: People whose information needs are supposed to be answered by the database.

Value of an attribute: A string of symbols that represents an attribute of a particular entity or relationship.

INDEX

DATE DUE